# CUMBRIA

# CUMBRIA

ROBERT WOODHOUSE

The
History
Press

First published 2009

The History Press
The Mill, Brimscombe Port
Stroud, Gloucestershire, GL5 2QG
www.thehistorypress.co.uk

British Library Cataloguing in Publication Data.
A catalogue record for this book is available from the British Library.

ISBN 978 0 7509 5078 7

Typesetting and origination by The History Press
Printed in Great Britain

# Contents

*Acknowledgements*                                    6

*Introduction*                                        7

*Visiting the Curiosities*                            8

1.   Carlisle and the Border Country                  9

2.   Northern Lakes                                   21

3.   Penrith and the Eden Valley                      40

4.   Southern Lakes (Coastal Strip)                   60

5.   Southern Lakes (Inland)                          87

*Bibliography*                                       127

# Acknowledgements

Researching and composing material from such a wide geographical area has inevitably involved a considerable amount of travel and research. A great deal of assistance was provided both before and during visits by tourist information centres at Cockermouth, Keswick, Windermere, Penrith, Grange-over-Sands, Egremont, Kendal, Sedbergh, Kirkby Lonsdale and Alston.

Apart from the author's own collection of books, articles and press cuttings, information was gathered from local history departments at several libraries including Grange-over-Sands, Barrow-in-Furness and Alston. Similar assistance with written material has been provided by staff at the Storr's Hall Hotel, Windermere; the Mortal Man Inn, Troutbeck; the Albion Inn, Arnside; the Tullie House Museum, Carlisle; the National Trust; clergy at St Cuthbert's Church, Carlisle; and staff at the Rheged Centre, near Penrith.

Even with a map references, some locations remained difficult to discover and it was on many such occasions that traditional Northern warmth and co-operation was in evidence. This was particularly the case at Arnside, Workington, Kendal as well as at St Bees, where school staff offered considerable assistance with research at the church.

A particular and special word of thanks must be given to Cedric Robinson, Queen's Guide to the Sands, for material on Morecambe Bay; Mr R.H. Thomas, for information about the Sedbergh School Synchronome; and Rob and Ralph Merrett for making available various materials (written and visual) from the Crab Fair Archive at Egremont.

Thanks are also due to Sandra Mylan for typing and administrative services. Few undertakings of this nature can be satisfactorily completed alone and I owe a large debt of gratitude to my wife, Sally, who has sustained boundless measures of patience and enthusiasm in fulfilling a number of roles ranging from driver, navigator and map reader to research assistant and proof reader.

# Introduction

The area covered by Cumbria includes the old counties of Cumberland and Westmorland, along with small sectors of the former Yorkshire and Lancashire county set-ups. At the heart of this north-western region of England are the mountains and lakes that attract a range of visitors from home and abroad, while lowland tracts are fringed by the Scottish border (to the north), the Irish Sea (on the west and southern edges) and the spreading peaks of the Pennines (away to the east).

With few major towns and cities among this arrangement of magnificent natural settings, it is perhaps surprising to find such a variety of oddities within Cumbria's boundaries.

Dramatic natural features such as the tidal bore in Morecambe Bay, the plunging Helm Wind on the slopes of Cross Fell and the dramatic bulk of the Bowder Stone provide an appropriate setting for countless man-made curiosities. Our early ancestors created the amazing stone circles at Castlerigg (near Keswick) and Long Meg and Her Daughters (north of Penrith), along with ancient crosses at Bewcastle and Irton and the incredible cat-eating bears at Dacre.

Different phases of church building have provided a range of unusual design features including the double aisles of Kendal's Holy Trinity Church, the tiny place of worship at Wasdale Head and Cartmel Priory's curiously-aligned tower.

Apart from the usual reminders of the area's industrial past in the form of housing and associated buildings, there are the dramatic and distinctive outlines of Whitehaven's Candlestick Chimney and the tower beside castellated chimneys at Castle Pit Head in Workington. In more rural parts there are the fascinating tales linked with hostelries, such as the Mortal Man, the Drunken Duck and the Golden Rule.

This area is also home to the highly unusual Herdwick breed of sheep and perhaps the strangest of all competitions, the gurning contest, which features at Egremont's annual crab fair.

*Robert Woodhouse, 2009*

# Visiting the Curiosities

The curiosities covered in this book are to be found in a whole range of locations. Several are landmarks and these are probably best viewed from a distance (especially when close inspection may involve a demanding ascent). A number are privately owned (as domestic or business premises) and must be viewed from the roadside, while some are subject to normal opening times. During the summer months several of the properties are opened on a limited basis and details are usually available from local tourist information centres.

The curiosities can be visited either singly or in groups. A few are in fairly remote countryside and can only be reached on foot, but the large majority are accessible by public transport.

Due care and attention should be exercised, in terms of traffic and on public roads, while caution is required at locations beside lakes and waterways.

one

# Carlisle and the
# Border Country

# BEWCASTLE CROSS

## *A MAJOR MONUMENT WITH SEVENTH-CENTURY ORIGINS*

**Access**

Bewcastle
is 25 miles
north-east of
Carlisle via the
B6318.

In a remote rural location to the north-east of Carlisle at Bewcastle is a collection of historic buildings, including a Roman camp, castle and medieval church of St Cuthbert, but pride of place in this fascinating back water must go to the magnificent churchyard cross.

Standing almost 15ft high, this four-sided sandstone column is covered in a variety of decorative detail. The north face has panels of vine, scrolls and knot work as well as a chequered panel, while the southern side includes a line of runes and part of a sundial which divides daylight into twelve parts. The eastern face has vine-scroll patterns with clusters of fruit, squirrels, birds and strange animals. It is, however, the west face that holds most interest. Three of the four panels are carved with human figures and show John the Baptist holding a holy lamb, Christ standing on a lion and an adder while his right hand is raised in blessing, and a man with a hawk on his wrist.

The head of the cross disappeared long ago and may have been taken to London in the early seventeenth century, but it is the finely-etched carvings that have caused endless debate among experts. It is now generally agreed that

Bewcastle Cross most probably dates from the seventh century AD and, although some detail has been worn away, most of the carving is exceptionally well preserved.

Along with Ruthwell Cross, from across the border in Scotland, this magnificent monument ranks as one of the finest examples of its type in Europe.

Bewcastle Cross in the churchyard of St Cuthbert's Church.

# MOVABLE PULPIT IN ST CUTHBERT WITHOUT, CARLISLE

## A MOBILE PREACHING POSITION

The church of St Cuthbert Without, which dates from the late 1770s, has a number of engaging features. Built of red and grey stone, its walls enclose a nave of eight bays, gallery supported on Tuscan columns, and a short, low chancel.

However, its most intriguing aspect must be the massive movable pulpit. It was manufactured in 1905 by locally based company Cowan & Sheldon, who specialised in constructing cranes and derricks. From its position at the side of the church, this huge item of furniture could be rolled on rails into a place at the west of the chancel. Ropes from the pulpit were fastened under the floor to a handle which was turned in the vestry. Once the sermon had been delivered and the preacher returned to his seat, the pulpit was transferred, on its rails, to its original position.

This splendid item of ecclesiastical equipment is still operated on about four occasions each year, but similar items are few and far between. There are some examples of movable organs which can be found at Sacred Trinity, Salford, St Paul's Church, Cheltenham, and St Andrew's, Glasgow.

**Access**

St Cuthbert Without is located on St Cuthbert's Lane, off the Market Place in Carlisle.

Movable pulpit in the Church of St Cuthbert Without, Carlisle.

Church of St Cuthbert Without, Carlisle.

# CITADEL RAILWAY STATION COATS OF ARMS

## *PIONEERING COMPANIES FROM THE EARLY DAYS OF STEAM LOCOMOTION*

**Access**

Carlisle railway station is at the south-west side of the city between the west of Botchergate and Court Square.

At one time no less than seven railway companies operated locomotives in and out of Carlisle, but when it came to making a decision about the main railway station it was the Caledonian Railway along with the Lancaster & Carlisle Railway that prevailed. They favoured the Citadel station site rather than other bases on London Road and Crown Street and it is their coats of arms that feature on the frontage of the station buildings.

Constructed during 1847–8, from designs by Sir William Tite, who was also the architect for the Bank of England, the station exterior incorporates a high arch and soaring clock tower.

Coats of arms of railway companies, Carlisle railway station.

# THE BISHOP'S STONE

## *A POWERFUL ECCLESIASTICAL DENUNCIATION*

A large white-painted boulder in the Tullie House Museum Millennium Subway provides a dramatic link with turbulent times in the border area some 500 years ago.

Standing around 7ft high, this massive stone is inscribed with part of the Archbishop of Glasgow's condemnation of the Border Reivers at a time when groups of sheep rustlers and robbers spread fear throughout the area. During 1525 this article of interdiction was proclaimed by priests from their church pulpits:

> I curse thair heid and all the haris of thair heid; I curse thair face, thair ane, thair mouth, thair neise, their toung, their teith, thair crag, thair schulderis, thair breist, thair hert, thair stomok, thair bak, thair wame, thair armes, thair leggis, thair handis, thair feit and everilk part of thair body, frae the top of thair heid to the soill of thair feit, befoir and behind, within and without.

**Access**

The Bishop's Stone is sited in the Tullie House Museum Millennium subway that links the museum with Carlisle Castle.

The Bishop Stone in the subway between the Tullie House Museum and Carlisle Castle.

This remarkable feature was installed in the subway as part of the Carlisle Gateway Project, but in recent times it has been given the unofficial title of 'the Cursing Stone' and has been blamed for a range of adversities including the foot and mouth outbreak, unemployment and local floods.

# FIDDLEBACK FARM

### *HUSBANDRY WITH A MUSICAL THEME*

**Access**

Fiddleback Farm and nearby arch are close to the village of Curthwaite, on the A595, south of Thursby.

While the majority of farm buildings have an easily recognisable plan, the overall layout of Fiddleback Farm, south of Thursby (near Carlisle) is highly unusual. The round farmhouse merges into a round barn to produce the shape of a fiddle or a figure of eight. The date '1709' is carved into a door lintel.

A nineteenth-century owner of this curiously-shaped property is said to have given it the title 'Fiddlecase Hall' and a curved feature above the entrance

*Above:* Fiddleback
Farm near
Curthwaite.

*Right:* Roadside
archway, close to
Fiddleback Farm
(beside the A595).

has the appearance of a musical note. (The black edging around the windows
and the Gothic-style front door are thought to have been added later.)

Within 100yds of the farm, beside the A595, stands an imposing stone-built
archway. It could be taken for the entrance to an impressive country house, but
in fact it is set in splendid isolation spanning a quiet country lane signposted
to Crofton.

Market Cross
at Brampton.

# BRAMPTON MARKET CROSS

## *OCTAGONAL MEMORIAL TO AN ABSTEMIOUS ARISTOCRAT*

**Access**

The market cross is at the centre of Brampton which is 6 miles north-east of Carlisle on the A69.

Brampton nestles in the picturesque Irthing Valley at the intersection of several routes. The cobbled market place has been the setting for a weekly (Wednesday) market ever since a charter was granted in 1252. At its centre stands an elaborate octagonal market cross known as the Howard Memorial Shelter (built in 1922).

It was built to commemorate the life and career of George James Howard, 9th Earl of Carlisle, who died in 1911 and his wife, Rosalind Frances, who died in 1921. The Howards were staunch supporters of the temperance movement and are mainly remembered for closing all the inns on their estates in Yorkshire and Cumberland.

In recent years this curious eight-sided building has housed the town's tourist information centre.

# CALDBECK CHURCHYARD

## *TWO CONTRASTING CUMBRIAN CHARACTERS: JOHN PEEL AND MARY HARRISON*

Among the gravestones in Caldbeck's spreading St Kentigern's churchyard are the final resting places of two very different personalities, John Peel and Mary Harrison.

John Peel was born in 1777 and was a keen supporter of blood sports; he was said to have been hunting until two weeks before his death in 1854. Peel's exploits assumed legendary proportions during his lifetime and the song, 'D'ye ken John Peel' (written after his death) ensured that his name and feats lived on.

One of the longest hunts on record involved John Peel when he was based on the estate of Armathwaite Hall. The chase was over 70 miles and it is suggested that foxes in Peel's lifetime were larger and stronger than their modern counterparts. Greyish in colour, they could easily run a 50 mile chase.

**Access**

St Kentigern's Church is set in the centre of Caldbeck on the B5299 to the south-west of Carlisle.

The grave of John Peel in St Kentigern's churchyard at Caldbeck.

Some reports suggest that John Peel was a rowdy braggart who exaggerated his excellence at field sports. He married above his station, thwarting possible objections to the alliance with a hastily-arranged marriage at Gretna Green, and then socialised above his rank. (A reference in the song to a 'coat so gay' is a corruption of 'grey' – a locally-woven cloth.)

Not far from Peel's grave is the final resting place of Mary Harrison, the beautiful daughter of a local landlord who had the misfortune to bigamously marry a villain named James Hartfield. In 1803 he was convicted of forgery and hung on the banks of the River Eden in Carlisle.

Mary then met and married Richard Harrison, and after moving to Todcroft Farm at Caldbeck they raised a family of five children. Her life story was described in a poem by William Wordsworth and in recent years Melvyn Bragg has written a novel about her life.

# SARAH LOSH'S FOLLIES AT WREAY

## *OUTSTANDING WORK OF A FEMALE VICTORIAN ARCHITECT*

**Access**

Wreay is situated between the M6 and A6 on the south side of Carlisle.

In the early nineteenth century it was unknown for a woman to pursue a career as an architect, but several buildings in Wreay, including St Mary's Church, bear witness to the superb design skills of Miss Sarah Losh.

Her family owned much of the land around Wreay and during 1830 Sarah was able to channel her creative talents into designing local buildings. The roadside school is simple and undistinguished, but the adjacent schoolmaster's house has the distinction of being based on measurements of a 1,800-year-old property that Sarah had come across at Pompeii in 1817. The Sexton's cottage alongside the churchyard (before later additions) seems to be based on similar designs.

Other examples of Sarah Losh's work include a Tudor-style house at Langarth and the well head at St Nimian's in Brisco, but her finest piece of work is undoubtedly St Mary's Church. To a great extent it seems to reflect the basilicas that she had seen in Italy, but internal features and carvings reflect characteristics of the Arts and Crafts movement some fifty years before this style became widespread.

Inside the church there are two massive wooden lecterns of an eagle and a flapping pelican and a whole range of carved furnishings. Butterflies and flowers feature on a wonderfully decorative font while wooden pine cones appear as door handles and on pillars. These are in memory of Major William Thain, a friend of the Losh family, who was shot by a poisoned arrow in the Khyber Pass. He had previously sent Sarah a cone from which she had grown a tree.

*Above left:* A portrait of Sarah Losh in Wreay Church.

*Above right:* The west door of Wreay Church.

*Below:* The font in Wreay Church.

A crocodile on the south wall of Wreay Church.

External walls of the church are decorated with a stone serpent, a bat, dragon gargoyles, a crocodile and a turtle. The churchyard houses a sundial, a memorial cross and mortuary chapel (which is now in use as a shed). It represents an exact replica of St Perran's Oratory, which was excavated near Perranporth, Cornwall, in 1835.

All around this quiet Cumbrian village setting are examples of the outstanding architectural talent of Sarah Losh.

two

# Northern
# Lakes

# CUMBERLAND PENCIL MUSEUM, KESWICK

## *EVERYTHING ANYONE EVER WANTED TO KNOW ABOUT PENCILS*

**Access**

The Exhibition Centre at the Southey Works is on the west side of the A591 towards the northern end of Keswick.

Up and down the country there are museums to cover most aspects of our heritage but in terms of curiosity value few, if any, can rival the Pencil Museum at Keswick.

Pencils were first made in Keswick more than 400 years ago and the museum is set close to the imposing 1930s factory building. Displays explain the process involved in making the range of Derwent Fine Art Pencils and other exhibits include the world's largest pencil and a Second World War pencil that resembles a James Bond-style gadget.

Local deliveries are still made from an old-fashioned van, while a row of coloured pencils form the roadside fence on either side of the bus stop outside Frizington Library on the route between Egremont and Cockermouth.

Cumberland Pencil Museum at Keswick.

The van of the Cumberland Pencil Co. Ltd.

# CASTLERIGG STONE CIRCLE

## *AN INTRIGUING ARRANGEMENT OF STANDING STONES*

There is a total of fifteen sites containing megaliths and stone circles in Cumbria (with other similar locations now possibly covered over) giving rise to any number of explanations for their original construction.

Castlerigg Stone Circle stands on an area of open ground high above, and to the east of, Derwent Water. Although it is termed a 'circle', the thirty-eight huge stones form an oval-shaped ring measuring about 100ft across and it is unique for having within the oval a rectangular enclosure formed by ten more stones.

It is unclear why this arrangement of standing stones was set up or how the collection of massive boulders was moved into position. There are suggestions that it was used by Druids or even early Christians and may date back some 3,000 to 4,000 years.

**Access**

Castlerigg Stone Circle is on the route between Goosewell and Castlerigg about 2 miles east of Keswick.

Castlerigg Stone Circle, near Keswick.

Candlestick Chimney from Whitehaven harbour.

Candlestick Chimney, Whitehaven.

# A CANDLESTICK CHIMNEY AND CASTELLATED MINE SHAFTS

## *FANCIFUL INDUSTRIAL BUILDINGS AT WHITEHAVEN*

Until the mid-1980s the recent industrial history of Cumbria's coastal strip was dominated by deep coal mining. A total of 120 pits were set up and some had workings spreading as far as 5 miles below the Irish Sea.

**Access**

The Candlestick Chimney and castellated mine shafts overlook Whitehaven harbour at the centre of the town.

Many of the eighteenth-century colliery buildings were erected by the 1st Earl of Lonsdale and a large number have the characteristics of castles. On high ground above the harbour stands a farmhouse which has been preserved as a memorial to the 100 miners who died in an underground explosion in 1910. A tall chimney dominates the town's harbour. Shipments of coal and iron ore during the eighteenth century saw Whitehaven ranked as the third busiest port in England and, as if to add a touch of levity to this bustling industrial setting, Lord Lonsdale had the chimney designed in the shape of a candlestick. Rather than functioning as an outlet for smoke emissions, it served as a ventilation shaft for mine workings.

Workington's Castle Pit Head.

# WORKINGTON'S CASTLE PIT HEAD

## *ROMANTIC REMINDERS OF AN EARLIER INDUSTRY*

A circular tower and two tall, castellated chimneys overlooking a playing field and housing estate are an unlikely reminder of Workington's industrial past. Known collectively as 'the Castle', they now stand in splendid isolation with the only hint of the hectic day-to-day activity that took place around their walls being an inscription 'ESC Esq. 1844' on the tall chimney. In fact this location was the entrance to Jane Pit, where coal-mining operations began in 1844.

Across the road was the entrance to another colliery, Annie Pit, which closed because of problems with subsidence and is now covered by the Territorial Army building.

**Access**

Castle Pit Head is on the south side of Workington, close to the Territorial Army building.

Workington's Castle Pit Head.

Spinning galleries
at Hartsop.

# SPINNING GALLERIES AT HARTSOP

## INTRIGUING REMINDERS OF HOME-BASED INDUSTRY

**Access**

Hartsop village
is close to
the southern
end of the
Kirkstone Pass
(about 10
miles north of
Windermere).

On most occasions it is the local church or hall that attracts the attention of visitors seeking out building of interest, but in some cases it is more humble structures that catch the eye. Close to the southern end of Kirkstone Pass, Hartsop Hall, a sixteenth-century manor house which has been adapted as a farmstead, is of interest because at an earlier date the building was inexplicably extended across an ancient right of way.

A little distance away, the tiny village of Hartsop has an intriguing throwback to an early cottage industry in the form of three houses with spinning galleries under the overhanging eaves. Before the Industrial Revolution, work was carried out in the home. Women spun thread on machines in the gallery, from which they then produced woven cloth in other areas of the house.

The Old Smoke House
at High Lorton.

# THE OLD SMOKE HOUSE, HIGH LORTON

## *INDUSTRIAL PREMISES WITH A TOUCH OF ANTIQUITY*

Tucked away behind a roadside wall, this charming circular tower has the look of an outbuilding linked to a castle or Gothic-style mansion. Decorative stonework at the upper level and an iron-framed roof give little indication that it was in use during the nineteenth century as a smoke house where ham and fish were cured over an oak fire.

Local residents held such affection for this curious Grade II listed building that they campaigned for its restoration during the early 1990s and this was achieved with financial assistance from the National Park Authority.

**Access**

High Lorton is on the B5292 to the south of Cockermouth.

The Bowder Stone in Borrowdale Valley.

# THE BOWDER STONE

*DRAMATIC EVIDENCE OF THE POWER OF GLACIAL ACTION*

**Access**

South of Keswick on the B5289 and half way up the Borrowdale Valley. A 600m pathway is well signposted from the public road.

The incredible range of landscape features throughout the Lake District were moulded by the action of glacial ice which scoured and ground its way across the land to form corries and steep-sided valleys. One of the most dramatic reminders of this episode is Borrowdale's Bowder Stone.

Advancing glaciers must have moved this enormous rock along as if it were a tiny pebble, only to leave it balanced precariously on a narrow edge where it has remained for over 500,000 years. Properly described as a 'Glacial Erratic', the Bowder Stone weighs around 2,000 tons and measures 60ft in length and 35ft in height.

Such is its balanced state that it is possible to shake hands with another person beneath the stone through a gap at its base while a ladder facilitates a climb to the peak in order to take in the spectacular views all round. The overhanging face of this remarkable rock is also popular with members of the rock-climbing fraternity.

The Butter Bell at
No. 7 Market Place,
Cockermouth.

# BUTTER BELL AT COCKERMOUTH

## *A RELIC FROM EARLIER DAYS OF MARKET TRADING*

Cockermouth has a number of buildings, statues and plaques with reminders of people from the town's past. These range from Mary, Queen of Scots (who took refuge in the home of Henry Fletcher after her defeat near Glasgow), to William Wordsworth (who was born and brought up in the town during the late eighteenth century). With such an array of prominent features it is easy to overlook less obvious curiosities such as the butter bell, which is set in an opening high on the wall of No. 7 Market Place. It was rung for many years on market days, when butter was one of the dairy products on sale.

**Access**

No.7 Market
Place,
Cockermouth.

# DACRE CASTLE, CHURCH AND CHURCHYARD CARVINGS

## *MYSTERIOUS FELINE CREATURES IN A DELIGHTFUL CHURCHYARD SETTING*

**Access**

Dacre is 2 miles north of Pooley Bridge and Ullswater and 5 miles south-west of Penrith.

Even the tiniest of villages boast buildings of great interest. Dacre was probably the site of a monastery between the seventh and tenth centuries, although no trace of it now remains. There is, however, ample evidence of this location's importance in the shape of Dacre Castle and St Andrew's Church.

Dacre Castle originated as an early fourteenth-century pele tower during the time of border warfare and although it fell into disrepair in more settled times, it was restored in 1675 by the Earl of Sussex. (It is now privately owned and not open to the public.)

St Andrew's Church is said to stand on the site of the Saxon monastery and a number of pre-Norman items of stonework are displayed within the building. Tiny thirteenth-century lancet windows and the square-headed priest door in the chancel are worth noting, but it is the adjacent churchyard that attracts most attention.

Apart from memorials to the Hassell family the most prominent features in the churchyard are four stone bears. They are said to mark the four corners of the original churchyard, but further meaning to their design is open to wide interpretation. Often referred to as the cat-eating bears, they

may illustrate episodes from the life of a bear. The first carving depicts the bear asleep; then with a cat clinging to his back; next trying to get rid of the cat and finally with his annoying visitor safely swallowed. Or, then again, they may just be the creations of a teasing stonemason. Though now badly eroded by weathering, they still tantalise and intrigue visitors to this delightful setting. It is believed that they were originally pinnacles on the walls of the gatehouse at nearby Dacre Castle.

St Andrew's Church, Dacre. Note the stone bear in the foreground.

Dacre churchyard stone bear (the first in the series – the bear asleep).

Dacre churchyard stone bear (the second in the series – a cat clings to the bear).

Dacre churchyard stone bear (the third in the series – the bear tries to dislodge the cat).

Dacre churchyard stone bear (the fourth in the series – the cat is swallowed).

# ONE-HANDED CLOCK ON KESWICK MOOT HALL

## *NO EXCUSE FOR POOR TIME KEEPING*

**Access**

The Moot Hall is in the centre of Keswick market square.

With its central location in the market square, Keswick's Moot Hall has long been a focal point of gatherings. The present building dates from 1813 (and houses the town's information centre), but earlier structures on the site were used as a court house and for market stalls. An end tower has a number of interesting features, including what appears to be a one-handed clock dating from 1601 in the upper section.

Closer inspection reveals that the other hand is, in fact, in position although it has been painted black so that it cannot be seen against the background. The reason for this arrangement seems to be linked with the fact that the clock, bell and working parts were removed from Lord's Island on nearby Derwent Water and re-assembled here. Common concensus seems to that in those earlier times, time-keeping was not such a precise art because the pace of life did not require minute by minute definition.

The one-handed clock on Keswick Moot Hall.

A close up of the one-handed clock at Keswick.

# A TRIO OF FAMOUS LOCAL SONS FROM EAGLESFIELD

## *ROBERT EGLESFIELD, FLETCHER CHRISTIAN AND JOHN DALTON*

The tiny village of Eaglesfield, located three miles south-west of Cockermouth, is remembered as the birthplace of three men who made headlines in very different walks of life.

Robert Eglesfield left this rural backwater to found Queen's College at Oxford University in the fourteenth century, while Fletcher Christian was born and brought up in the locality during the mid-eighteenth century before following a career at sea that culminated in his leading the infamous mutiny on the *Bounty*.

John Dalton's career took a very different route during the pioneering days of scientific investigation. Born in 1766 into a Quaker family of farmers, he left school at the age of ten, but soon excelled as a teacher and became professor of mathematics and natural philosophy at New College, Manchester.

**Access**

The village of Eaglesfield is 3 miles south-west of Cockermouth. The Dalton Plaque is above a wooden door on a white-painted house in the centre of the village and Fletcher Christian's birthplace is marked by a plaque at Moorland Close Farm just outside the village.

*Above:* The birthplace of John Dalton at Eaglesfield.

JOHN DALTON. DCL. LLD.
THE DISCOVERER OF
THE ATOMIC THEORY
WAS BORN HERE SEPT 5 1766
DIED AT MANCHESTER JULY 27 1844

*Left:* The plaque on the cottage at Eaglesfield.

He made importance discoveries relating to gases, the force of steam and the elasticity of vapours, before delivering the initial results of his inquiry into 'the relative weights of the ultimate particles' to the Manchester Philosophical Society at the age of thirty-seven. During the following year Dalton produced his theory of atomic weights, where he took hydrogen as the unit in order to formulate twenty-one atomic weights, each of which was expressed in terms of hydrogen. This effectively opened up a new area of scientific research.

John Dalton died at Manchester on 27 July 1844 and a simple inscribed tablet on a small white-painted house in Eaglesfield marks the village's connection with this remarkable man of science.

Waterworks at Thirlmere.

# WATERWORKS AT THIRLMERE

## *CASTELLATED OUTLINES OF A MUNICIPAL ENTERPRISE*

An imposing building beside Lake Thirlmere looks in every respect like an impressive North Country castle. Turrets, battlements and a painted crest give every appearance of a genuine baronial seat, but in fact it is the Manchester Corporation Waterworks.

The scheme was approved by the city council in 1877 and authorised by an Act of Parliament two years later, but it was 1894 before the building was completed. A large plaque on one wall lists the chairmen and deputy chairmen of the council who were involved in this prestigious project.

**Access**

The water-works is located on the shoreline of Lake Thirlmere on the A591 between Ambleside and Keswick.

# FARM BUILDINGS AT GREYSTOKE

## *FANCIFUL FEATURES AND UNUSUAL NAMES IN A RURAL SETTING*

A group of three follies close to the village of Greystoke have a whole range of whimsical features disguising the fact that they are actually farmhouses. Dating from the late eighteenth century, external aspects including pillars, castellations, turrets, pointed arches and a tall, Gothic window give two of these follies an appearance of forts; this connection is continued in their names – Bunkers Hill and Fort Putnam (after General Israel 'Puffing' Putnam). The third folly, Spire House, has the look of a church, while a fourth property 'Jefferson' has no decorative features, but continues links with the American War of Independence.

**Access**

The farm buildings are on the north side of the A66 between Greystoke and Penrith. (They are privately owned with no access to the public.)

Fort Putham at Greystoke.

Bunker's Hill at Greystoke.

Spire House at Greystoke.

These highly unusual farm buildings were built for the 11th Duke of Norfolk, but the identity of the architect is unclear. Francis Horne was staying at Greystoke in 1787 and may well have been responsible for the constructions as he completed various projects for the duke including alterations to Arundel Castle and the triangular folly Horne's Tower. It is also thought that the duke himself may have been the architect with Francis Horne acting in an advisory role.

The reason for construction of these curious rural edifices is something of a mystery; one suggestion is that they were in fact built to irritate the Duke of Norfolk's Tory neighbour, the Earl of Lonsdale.

# WATENDLATH

### *A CANDIDATE FOR THE COUNTRY'S MOST SECLUDED SETTLEMENT*

England's northern uplands have any number of isolated settlements, but among contenders for the remotest village, Watendlath must rank very near the top of the list.

Leaving the B5289 road between Borrowdale and Derwent Water, it takes a further 3 miles along the narrowest of country lanes with endless bends to reach this fascinating location. Along the way there is a magnificent vantage point at 'Surprise View' with panoramas in both directions along the lower valley and a renowned single-span packhorse bridge, Ashness Bridge.

**Access**

Watendlath is 3 miles east of the B5289 between Borrowdale and Derwent Water.

Picturesque Watendlath.

The tiny settlement of Watendlath lies close to a small lake and in the shadow of the 2,000ft summit of High Seat. In recent years all the properties apart from one (which is privately owned) have passed to the ownership of the National Trust.

In earlier days Sir Hugh Seymour Walpole moved to these parts and was based at Brackenburn while he wrote the *Hernes Chronicles*, which were set in Watendlath.

The approach to a small footbridge over a beck beside the village has a curious stone that was placed there to mark a visit by HRH the Prince of Wales.

# HERDWICK SHEEP

## *A DISTINCTIVE BREED WITH PROBABLE SCANDINAVIAN ORIGINS*

**Access**

Herdwick sheep are found in many upland areas of the Lake District but most notably in central and western areas (including Watendlath).

Most town-dwellers can probably recognise few differences in the appearance of the flocks of sheep that graze remote rural slopes, but since the late nineteenth century distinct breeds have been developed by Cumbrian communities.

The Rough Fell breed has long whitish fleece, black-and-white speckled face, 'Roman nose' and short horns, while Swaledales have short, cream-coloured fleece, white nose on a black face and curled horns. The hardiest of all breeds, however, is the distinctive Herdwick breed.

Nowadays, Herdwick sheep are usually found in central and western areas of the Lake District, but in earlier times they could be seen over a much wider area ranging from Caldbeck in the north to Low Furness in the south and eastwards to Shap and Kentmere.

The Herdwick is an exceptionally sturdy sheep, capable of living on the most rugged of landscapes with sparse vegetation and the country's highest levels of rainfall. Their distinctive grey fleece, white heads and sturdy legs make them easily recognisable and it is the dense fleece, which dries out more quickly than other breeds, that helps them to exist in more remote settings.

Although there is no clear evidence that the Herdwick has Scandinavian origins, it its known that Viking settlers from the ninth century kept large numbers of sheep on the fells and the name is derived from 'herd-vik' (Old Norse for 'sheep farm').

Herdwick meat is famed for its tasteful quality and moves have been made to prevent inferior meats being substituted for 'Lakeland Herdwick'. On the other hand its fleece has very little value for woollen fabrics, although there has been recent success in producing hard-wearing carpets.

The National Trust owns a large number of fell farms in the central and western dales and leases to tenants around 25,000 Herdwick sheep. In recent

*Above & below:* Herdwick sheep.

years a number of patrons including Beatrix Potter, Professor G.M. Trevelyan and Lake District Farm Estates have passed Herdwick farms to the National Trust so that a total of about 150 farms, including privately owned operations, are currently breeding Herdwick sheep on a commercial basis.

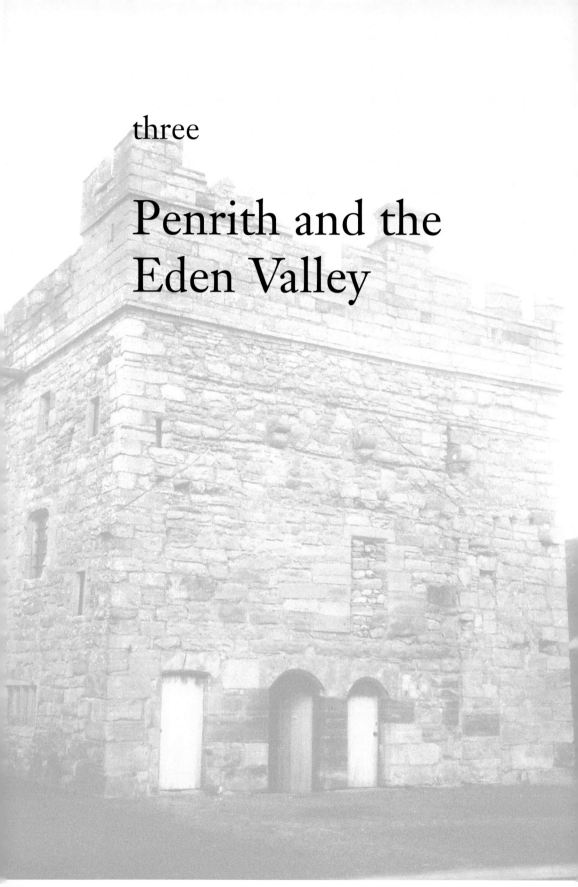

three

# Penrith and the
# Eden Valley

# LONG MEG AND HER DAUGHTERS

## *STRANGE ARRANGEMENTS OF LARGE MAN-MADE STONE RINGS*

Cumbria has more than fifteen sites where standing stones are clearly visible and one of the best preserved is located near Little Salkeld, a few miles north-east of Penrith. Measuring some 400yds in circumference and made up of a total of fifty-nine stones, Long Meg and her Daughters is the second largest stone circle in England (after Stonehenge).

Originally there were about seventy stones made up of different types of rock, with greenstone, limestone and granite forming the majority. 'Long Meg' is the name attached to a tapering stone which is about 18ft high and 15ft around the base with a likely weight of about 17 tons. It stands a few yards away from the large circle. Close by are four 'daughters' who, together with their taller stone neighbour, form a gateway entrance to the main site. Cup and ring markings on Long Meg's surface are thought to have been carved more than 4,000 years ago.

The oval arrangement of stones is surrounded by an earth-and-stone bank and, inevitably, this amazing site is surrounded by folklore. One fanciful account suggests that Long Meg was a local witch who was turned to stone along with her daughters for 'profaning the Sabbath with wild dancing', but a more likely explanation is that the tallest stone was named after a genuine character, Meg of Malden, who lived in the area during the seventeenth

**Access**

Long Meg and her Daughters stone circle is close to Little Salkeld, about 6 miles north-east of Penrith via A686.

Long Meg near Little Salkeld.

Long Meg and her Daughters.

century. There is even a suggestion that Long Meg has magical properties and if an onlooker is able to count the same number of stones twice then Long Meg will spring to life or even Old Nick himself will put in an appearance.

# MAYBURGH HENGE AND KING ARTHUR'S ROUND TABLE

## *GATHERING PLACES FOR OUR EARLY ANCESTORS*

**Access**

Mayburgh Henge is at Eamont Bridge just south of Penrith on the A6.

This site is unusual in terms of British henge monuments because it does not include a perimeter ditch. A roughly circular bank standing at 8–15ft high is made up of pebbles from nearby water-courses and encloses about 1½ acres of ground.

The site is 130yds in diameter and in the centre of it stands a single upright stone measuring about 10ft in height. Until the nineteenth century there were three more stones in the central area and two pairs beside the entrance on the eastern side.

About a ¼ mile to the east are the remains of King Arthur's Round Table, which measures 300ft in diameter with an external bank about 5ft high. Until the seventeenth century two standing stones stood outside the northern entrance, but disturbance during the 1800s has destroyed many of the features.

Among various explanations for these henges are the possibilities that they were used as temples or as a meeting place for a large prehistoric district.

The upright stone at the centre of Mayburgh Henge.

Mayburgh Henge and the external bank of King Arthur's Round Table.

# THE COUNTESS PILLAR

## *A LINK WITH THE POWERFUL CLIFFORD FAMILY*

The Clifford family were a major force in the North Country for several centuries and in 1651 Lady Anne Clifford began a major programme of repair and rebuilding on family estates at Appleby, Brough, Pendragon, Skipton and Brougham.

Born at Skipton Castle in 1590, she took up residence at Brougham Castle in 1649 and arranged the restoration of numerous churches as well as family-owned castles. (In 1655 she repaired Appleby Church and built her own vault, in which she was buried following her death at Brougham Castle in 1676.)

On the south side of the A66, some 2 miles from the castle, stands the Countess Pillar which resembles a market cross. It was erected by Lady Anne Clifford in 1656 in memory of her 'good and pious' mother who died some forty years earlier. It is an octagonal pillar with a cubed upper block topped by a shortened pyramid-shaped roof and finial. Three sides of the block display sundials painted in bright blue and gold, while the other face is engraved with two coats of arms and a skull.

Below the sundial on the south side is an inscription requesting that an annuity of £4 should be distributed to poor people of the parish. The custom continues today with a ceremony on 2 April each year.

**Access**

The Countess Pillar stands beside the A66, east of Penrith, some 2 miles east south-east of Brougham Castle.

The Countess Pillar on the south side of the A66 near Penrith.

The tablet on the Countess Pillar.

Sundials on the Countess Pillar.

# THE CHINESE DOOR-KNOCKER, BROUGHAM HALL

## *RE-CREATING EARLIER EXAMPLES OF CRAFTSMANSHIP*

Brougham Hall, near Eamont Bridge, has had an eventful history. From humble beginnings as a small pele tower, it was later enlarged by Lord Brougham and Vaux, inventor of the Brougham carriage, into the 'Windsor of the North', but then became derelict during the 1930s.

In 1985 an extensive restoration scheme got underway to provide workshops and showrooms in refurbished stables and servants' quarters around the perimeter wall. A cast-iron door-knocker hung on the Great West Door until 1952 when it was stolen. Efforts to produce a replacement were unsuccessful for more than forty years. During 1993 a bronze founder in Sussex was able to fashion a copy of the knocker from photographs, and this splendid example of craftsmanship again adorns the Great West Door to Brougham Hall.

**Access**

Brougham Hall is 2 miles south-east of Penrith, close to the A6 (near Eamont Bridge).

Chinese door-knocker, Brougham Hall.

# RHEGED

## *'THE VILLAGE ON THE HILL' LINKING EARLIER TIMES WITH THE PRESENT AND FUTURE IN LAKELAND*

Opened on 4 August 2000 by Lord Melvyn Bragg, Rheged represents an important element in the establishment of tourist-orientated projects at the northern gateway to the English Lakes. An initial phase of the overall project dates from 1970 when a group of local entrepreneurs formed Westmorland Motorway Services and subsequent stages included construction of a hotel, caravan site and truck stop.

During the late 1990s Westmorland bought the land at Rheged, which had planning permission for a hotel, and set out to reflect the spirit of the Lake District and encourage visitors to discover areas of Cumbria and the North Pennines. At the heart of this innovative venture is a large-format cinema, with one of this country's largest screens to show the film *Rheged and the Lost Kingdom*. Supporting this visual presentation are shops that specialise in local produce, working craftsmen, restaurants, a conference centre, exhibition areas and education centre. The whole project covers 91,000 sq.ft, on five different levels, and a complete covering of turf makes it Europe's largest grass-covered building. In order to ensure that Rheged has the look of an actual Lakeland hill, moulds were made from limestone crags on Shap Fell and then used to recreate Rheged's own rocky features.

**Access**

Rheged is close to the M6 (Junction 40) at Penrith.

The main entrance to the Rheged Centre.

The grass-covered roof on the Rheged Centre.

The Grade II listed lime-kilns at Rheged.

Two nearby lakes feed a pair of waterfalls and a stream inside the main building, while a set of Grade II listed limekilns have been restored to form a central focus for this £18 million venture. The main entrance to Rheged has been designed to reflect features of a lime kiln and the doors are constructed from 'Float Glass' which resembles frozen water.

The name 'Rheged' is derived from the name of an ancient kingdom of Cumbria during the Dark Ages and its setting within a former limestone quarry provides a link with recent industrial activity but, above all, this splendid project provides a summary of the wide ranging appeal offered by the English Lake District.

# PENRITH'S STREET SIGNS

## *CLUES IN STONE TO A TOWN'S VARIED PAST*

Penrith's town centre streets have many interesting buildings and an enchanting atmosphere that invites closer investigation. The former William Robinson's School, Hutton Hall and the George Hotel all help to create charming locations that are enriched by a number of fascinating street signs.

**Access**

Penrith town centre.

Typical of these intriguing stone tablets is the lamb on the wall over the arched gateway to Crown Terrace, off King Street. It is displayed above the date 1776 at the entrance to a former wool merchant's hall and serves as a reminder of the days when Penrith was an important centre for the woollen industry.

The stone tablet above the entrance to the wool merchant's hall in Penrith.

*Above & below:* Street signs in Penrith.

# INTRIGUING MEMORIALS TO MIGHTY MEN OF THE PAST

## *THE 'GIANT'S THUMB' AND 'GIANT'S GRAVE'*

Apart from the west tower, the main body of St Andrew's Church at Penrith dates from the early 1720s and its red sandstone walls make an impressive backdrop for a number of much older stones which probably date from before 1000 AD.

The 'Giant's Thumb' is an Anglo-Saxon cross which may date from the mid-tenth century AD and has a wheel-type head with interlacing on its sides. It is in a prominent position on the north-west side of the west tower.

The 'Giant's Grave' is composed of two crosses of red sandstone with four sides of hogback coffins between the end stones. Both upright stones are round at the tower end of the shaft with square-sided upper sections. The western cross of the 'grave' stands over 11ft high and has interlaced work with a small cross head, while 15ft away the east cross is slightly shorter and has interlaced work showing a bound figure with a woman beside him and a serpent about his head. Above the serpent is the Agnus Dei.

The various items that make up this curious arrangement of stones are believed to date from the late tenth century AD.

Speculation suggests that the 'Giant's Grave' was originally assembled as a memorial to an earlier Cumbrian leader when a previous church was built on the site during the Norman period.

**Access**

St Andrew's Church is located in the centre of Penrith.

The 'Giant's Grave' in St Andrew's churchyard, Penrith.

The 'Giant's Thumb', an Anglo-Saxon cross in St Andrew's churchyard.

# CLIFTON HALL

## *ECHOES OF EARLIER GLORIES IN A FARMYARD SETTING*

**Access**

Within the collection of farm buildings at Clifton on the south side of Penrith via A66.

By 1173 Gilbert d'Engaine was a celebrated member of Westmorland gentry and owned Clifton Hall. His descendants continued to live here for several hundred years until the manor passed to the Wybergh family. During the mid-seventeenth century they accrued heavy debts and their lands were purchased by a neighbouring landowner, Sir John Lowther.

During the nineteenth century farm buildings were constructed around the only surviving portion of Clifton Hall – the fifteenth-century tower. Two doorways on the south wall indicate where the hall range was attached and on the east side large windows were inserted at three different levels during the eighteenth century.

The tower has been managed by English Heritage since 1973 and is reached by a footpath that runs from the public road beside the farm buildings.

*Above:* Clifton Hall – a fifteenth-century tower and nineteenth-century farm buildings.

*Right:* Clifton Hall.

**15th-century manor house**

Illustration showing how the first floor chamber may have looked in about 1600

The tower of Clifton Hall dates from about 1500. It is all that remains of a manor house which was begun in about 1400, then added to and altered over the next 400 years. Early in the 19th century the nearby farmhouse was built and most of the old hall was demolished, except the remaining tower.

*Left:* The information board at Clifton Hall.

*Below:* The upper floor of Clifton Hall.

# THE HELM WIND

## A MIGHTY BLAST FROM MOORLAND WASTES

Upland slopes around Cross Fell's flat-topped summit are the gathering ground for Britain's most powerful wind; the Helm Wind. From the upper reaches of Teesdale and Weardale this cold blast sweeps towards Cross Fell where it blows at right-angles to the scarp before suddenly plunging downwards in an icy blast. In meteorological terms such a wind is known as a 'Katabatic' wind, meaning 'one that drops'. Other less destructive examples can be found at Bluebell Hill in the North Down and in the Cotswolds.

Other features of Cumbria's Helm Wind are that it is often accompanied by some form of cloud cap or 'helmet' and at times the upper edge of the Helm takes on a shape that roughly corresponds with the contour of the Cross Fell range. The make-up of the 'helmet' indicates the nature of the blast, 'black' or 'white', of which the 'black' variety is the fiercer. This fearful gale is usually accompanied by a distinctive howl or roar.

Down the years a number of dramatic tales have been linked to an appearance of the Helm Wind. Some years ago bunches of hay were seen careering above Windermere at an estimated height of 2,000ft in the teeth of the Helm's might.

**Access**

Cross Fell is clearly visible from the A66 along the stretch to the north of Appleby.

The slopes of Great Dun Fell and course of the Tees.

On a regular basis trees have been uprooted and haycocks have been hoisted bodily and then dropped into an adjoining field. Wooden farm buildings on the western slopes of the Cross Fell range have often collapsed before the gale and with the wind in the opposite direction cyclists have found it impossible to cycle downhill. Other reports may be firmly placed in the realms of tall story telling and these include a report from the Middleton in Teesdale area about a man who was carrying a cross-cut saw under one arm when the 'Helum' – Helm Wind – blew out every other tooth of the saw. An Appleby man topped this tale by suggesting that a local blacksmith saw his forge blasted by this monstrous wind to such an extent that his anvil was lifted skywards and sent hurtling over a house top.

The widespread opinion is that 'a Helm Wind blows nobody good,' but earlier historical campaigns may provide a couple of intriguing exceptions. Could the western storms that scattered the Spanish Armada have been the malevolent Helm and was it a similar mighty gale that broke up invading Norman forces during an attack on Earl Boethar's English troops near Grasmere?

# THE CLOISTERS LEADING TO ST STEPHEN'S CHURCH, KIRKBY STEPHEN

## *CLASSICAL FEATURES AT A CHURCHYARD ENTRANCE*

**Access**

St Stephen's Church is at the northern end of Kirkby Stephen market place.

Set against a dramatic backdrop of Pennine slopes including Wildboar Fell and Hugh's Seat, Kirkby Stephen's streets are full of character and interest. Crooked little seventeenth-century houses stand alongside the quaint market hall and impressive Georgian and Victorian properties, but the town's crowning glory is the long, red sandstone church of St Stephen.

There are traces of Saxon and Norman stonework within the main body of the church, but it is the early sixteenth-century tower that has led to it being likened to a small cathedral.

The chancel and its chapels date from 1847 and this impressive structure also gained its grand entrance in the early nineteenth century. As befits a church building of this stature, an imposing set of cloisters serve as a screen between the market place and extensive churchyard. Built in 1810 by George Gibson, the eight Tuscan columns are arranged so that four project in front of the others and the upper section is topped by a bellcote.

The cloisters leading to St Stephen's Church, Kirkby Stephen.

# ALSTON'S TOWN HALL, MARKET CROSS, PARISH CHURCH AND UNDERGROUND TUNNEL

## *UNUSUAL FEATURES ABOVE AND BELOW GROUND AT ENGLAND'S HIGHEST MARKET TOWN*

Set on a hillside at about 1,000ft above sea level, Alston looks out across bleak slopes looped by roads that thread upwards towards the township. From the banks of the river steep lanes and open yards rise through the grey stonework of the old settlement that is often described as 'England's highest market town.'

At the lower level of the township, the Gothic-style Town Hall of 1857 has an impressive clock tower that illustrates Alston's earlier importance as a mining centre. Across the steeply sloping roadway the steeple of St Augustine's Church is a landmark for many miles. Fragments of Alston's medieval church are housed in the porch, but the main fabric dates from 1870.

**Access**

Alston is 20 miles north-east of Penrith via the Hartside Pass and 22 miles south-west of Hexham via the A686.

Alston market cross.

The central area of the market place is dominated by the market cross, which has Tuscan columns supporting a four-sided roof. The original cross was built in 1765 by Sir William Stephenson, but rebuilding work first took place in 1880 and again in 1968, following damage by a runaway lorry, before further repairs were carried out in 1980. Sir William Stephenson was born just outside Alston and spent his early years in the area before moving to the capital, where he became Lord Mayor in 1764.

Further up Front Street (and almost opposite the Society of Friends Meeting House) is Alston's fire station. Manned by retained fire fighters, it is one of the smallest in the country and is housed in a former grammar school building (of 1828).

Below the town, Nent Force marks the point on the South Tyne where John Smeaton began work in 1787 on an underground tunnel that ran 5 miles across open country to mine workings at Nenthead. (An inscribed stone in Alston town hall records this marvellous engineering achievement.)

The inscription on Alston market cross.

four

# Southern Lakes (Coastal Strip)

# GOSFORTH CROSS, THE FISHING STONE AND 'HOGBACKS'

## *TREASURED TENTH-CENTURY STONEWORK WITH NORSE/CHRISTIAN INTERPRETATIONS*

St Mary's Church at Gosforth dates largely from the late 1890s, but within its walls and in the adjacent churchyard are several examples of amazing Anglo-Saxon and Anglo-Danish work.

The sandstone Gosforth Cross stands almost 15ft high among gravestones in the churchyard and dates from the late ninth century. A rounded lower section gives way to a square upper part topped by a fine four-holed head carved with the emblem of the Trinity. Carvings on the lower portion of the cross are believed to represent the trunk and leaves of the World Ash, the sacred tree that was held to support the universe, while the upper part has a range of figures and designs symbolising the belief that the newly arrived faith, Christianity, would eventually triumph over paganism.

**Access**

Gosforth is on the A595 heading north from Ravenglass and Muncaster or from Eskdale and the Hardknott Pass.

Gosforth Cross in St Mary's churchyard.

The Fishing Stone in St Mary's Church, Gosforth.

The hogbacks in St Mary's Church, Gosforth.

At one time, there were three other similar crosses standing within the churchyard and although fragments of these have survived, the shafts have been lost long ago.

The Fishing Stone (now displayed inside St Mary's Church) was discovered in the churchyard in 1882 and represents an example of the way in which early Christian preachers used well-known Viking tales to convey a Christian theme. A plaited serpent motif runs across the centre of the stone with the top half showing a hart trampling a serpent (to indicate the triumph of good over evil) and lower section depicting Thor out fishing with the giant Hymir for the great Midgard serpent (an evil spirit) using the head of an ox as bait.

Experts believe that the Fishing Stone and 'hogbacks' in St Mary's Church are of the Urnes style from the later Viking period. It is likely that the hogbacks originally stood in the churchyard, where they served as tombstones. The Saint's Tomb is covered with assorted carvings of animal heads, with the figure of a man astride in the jaws of one of the beasts, and are said to illustrate the killing of the evil Fenris wolf by Vidar, in the final major battle of the Norse sagas between the forces of good and evil. The Warrior's Tomb has a battle scene showing two armies facing each other and carrying round shields as well as spears. It is said to indicate a truce between the two warring forces.

# CARTMEL PRIORY

## *UNUSUAL ARRANGEMENT OF THE CHURCH TOWER AND SPLENDID ORIGINAL FEATURES*

Cartmel Priory was founded in the late 1180s by William Marshall, Earl of Pembroke, to house Augustinian Canons. Built in the late Norman and Perpendicular Gothic style it was located in a backwater of the country and saw few official visits apart from Archbishop Wickwane of York, who made an official call during 1281.

Scottish raiders inflicted damage on the priory buildings in 1316 and 1322, but building work continued and the nave was completed during the mid-fifteenth century. Disaster struck in the mid-fifteenth century when the southern end of the domestic buildings collapsed, most probably because they had been constructed on the site of an Ice-Age lake.

The priory tower is claimed to be unique because the upper section is set at an angle of forty-five degrees on the lower section. This unusual arrangement is thought to have been made in order to prevent interior arches in the main body of the church from breaking outwards.

At ground-floor level, a door in the south-west corner has holes that are said to have been caused by village folk firing at Parliamentary troops in 1643, and inside the church a thirteenth-century choir stall and fifteenth-century east window with original stained glass attract interest. This splendid building continues in use as the parish church.

**Access**

Cartmel village lies north of the A590 some 4 miles from Grange-over-Sands.

The upper section of the tower at Cartmel Priory.

Cartmel Priory.

# CARTMEL RACECOURSE

*A SHORT, NARROW COURSE WITH THE LONGEST FINAL RUN-IN*

**Access**

The racecourse is slightly to the west of the central square at Cartmel.

The delightful village of Cartmel grew up around the twelfth-century priory, with a backdrop of rolling fields rising towards open moorland and fells. It is these spreading open sections of countryside that probably account for the presence of a national hunt racecourse within a few hundred yards of the central square. Covering a sharp, narrow oval-shaped circuit, the course has just six fences, but the 4-furlong run-in from the last fence is the longest in the United Kingdom.

Race meetings are held on spring and summer bank holiday weekends, but other events are staged in Racecourse Park throughout the year, with Cartmel Agricultural Show in early August a particular highlight.

# CARTMEL PRIORY GATEHOUSE

*A GLIMPSE OF EARLY MONASTIC OUTBUILDINGS*

**Access**

The grey-walled gatehouse faces on to Cartmel's central square.

Now isolated from the main body of the Priory Church of St Mary and St Michael, a fine fourteenth-century gatehouse faces the charming square

*Above:* Cartmel racecourse.

*Right:* Cartmel Priory gatehouse.

in the centre of Cartmel. An upper room, with access via a spiral staircase, served first as the manorial courtroom and then as a grammar school from the early seventeenth century through to the reign of King George III, before becoming a shop and function hall. Old stone faces are carved into the walls on either side of the vaulted archway that formerly led into the priory precincts.

In recent years this captivating building has been managed by the National Trust. It ranks as one of only around a hundred monastic gatehouses in the country to survive complete and unaltered.

# CAST-IRON OBELISK IN MEMORY OF JOHN WILKINSON

## *AN ENDURING MONUMENT TO THE 'IRON-MAD' ENGINEER*

**Access**

Lindale is south of the A590 (to the north of Grange-over-Sands) and 13 miles west of Kendal.

Castle Head, to the south-east of Lindale and overlooking the estuary of the River Kent, was the home of one of this country's pioneering iron makers. John Wilkinson's exploits earned him the title 'Iron-Mad' and among his achievements are the launching of the first iron ship and installation of the first large French steam engine. He accumulated such wealth and measure of importance that he had his own money coined and circulated during his lifetime.

After his death in 1808, he was buried, according to his own wishes, in an iron coffin in the garden of Castle Head. Over the next few years Wilkinson's coffin was moved no less than three times before it finally came to rest in Lindale churchyard.

A tall cast-iron obelisk near the centre of Lindale has enjoyed a similarly chequered history. Removed from Castle Head gardens in June 1863, it was deposited in a number of locations, including the River Winster, and following its re-erection close to the village it was badly damaged by lightning. A nationwide appeal raised funds for necessary repairs and in addition to a gold bust portrait of Wilkinson there is a lengthy inscription which reads:

John Wilkinson
Iron Master
Who died XIV July MDCCCVIII
Aged LXXX years
His different works
In various parts of the

Kingdom
Are lasting testimonies
Of his unceasing
Labours;
His life was spent in
Action
For the benefit
Of man;
And as he presumed
Humbly to hope
To the
Glory of God

And on the base of the plinth:

*Labore Et Honore*

The cast-iron
obelisk in
memory
of John
Wilkinson at
Lindale.

# ST ANTHONY'S TOWER, MILNTHORPE

## *A REMINDER OF A LEGISLATIVE LANDMARK*

**Access**

St Anthony's Tower is clearly visible on the north side of Milnthorpe, which lies some 12 miles west of Kirkby Lonsdale and close to the A6.

Until the arrival of the railways, Milnthorpe was Westmorland's only seaport and numbered among many ships registered at the port were *Eliza*, *The Isobel* and *The Dove*.

Those earlier days of coastal trading are long gone, but a nearby hilltop provides an interesting link with those times of commercial prosperity. St Anthony's Hill was given as part of the endowment of St Anthony's Chapel in Kendal parish church in 1500 and the small, round tower on the summit was built in the 1830s to celebrate the passing of the first parliamentary reform bill in 1832. This legislation from Earl Grey's government was the first stage in extending the right to vote to all adults, and St Anthony's Tower may possibly be unique in representing the only known monument to the Reform Act of 1832.

St Anthony's Tower at Milnthorpe.

# HOSPICE ON HAMPSFIELD FELL

## *A CLERIC'S FINE GESTURE TO TRAVELLERS*

High on the fells above Grange-over-Sands is a plain, square building that resembles a wartime pill box. In fact this curious, squat structure dates from 1846 when it was constructed by the vicar of Cartmel, Revd Thomas Remington, 'for the shelter and entertainment of travellers over the fell.'

Above the entrance is an inscription in Clarendon Greek and the simple interior, which has three benches around a small fireplace, has further words from Revd Remington:

> This hospice of Hampsfield is an open door, a like to welcome rich and poor,
> a roomy seat for young and old, where they may screen from the cold.
> Three windows that command a view, to north, to west and southward too
> a flight of steps requireth care, the roof will show a prospect rare.
> Mountain and vale you thence survey, the winding streams and noble bay
> the sun at noon the shadow hides, along the east and western sides.
> A lengthened chain holds guard around, to keep the cattle from the ground
> Kind reader freely take your pleasure, but do no mischief to my treasure.

An external stone staircase gives access to the roof where a moveable viewfinder is set within perimeter railings. From this vantage point there are magnificent views towards Old Man Coniston, Helvelyn and the Langdales on one side and Morecambe Bay on the other, while open heath land around the summit of the fell has fine examples of limestone paving.

**Access**

Hampsfield Fell is on the north side of Grange-over-Sands and close to the Cistercian Way, which links Cartmel to Grange.

The hospice on Hampsfield Fell, near Grange-over-Sands.

The rear of the hospice on Hampsfield Fell.

# THE FAIRY STEPS

## *DRAMATIC LIMESTONE FISSURE ON AN OLD CORPSE WAY*

**Access**

The Fairy Steps are about 1¼ miles along the Coffin Route, which starts on Black Dyke Road on the northern outskirts of Arnside.

Before St James' Church was completed in 1866 Arnside was included in the parish of Beetham. This meant a journey for worshippers of about 2½ miles along unmade paths and tracks, and the most direct route involved scaling the scarps of Winscar, on Beetham Fell, by an extremely narrow fissure known as the 'Fairy Steps'.

As it also featured as a coffin or 'corpse' route, it was necessary to raise coffins up the two scarps with ropes attached to the rock face through ring bolts. In more recent times further rings have been added by rock climbers scaling the vertical faces.

From the level summit above this slender opening there are fine views of Arnside Knott, the Kent estuary and the Lakeland Fells.

Fairy Steps near Arnside.

The narrow Fairy Steps.

'Underhill' and 'Underwood' on Arnside promenade.

# 'UNDERHILL' AND 'UNDERWOOD'

## FANCIFUL COTTAGES ON ARNSIDE PROMENADE

A range of domestic and business properties spread along Arnside's promenade overlooking Morecambe Bay. Many have been altered since their original construction during the nineteenth century, but a pair of whimsical cottages close to the junction with Ashleigh Road have retained their Victorian charm.

'Underhill' and 'Underwood' were built by the Barker family of Saltcotes Farm soon after the opening of Arnside's railway station in 1857. At that time they would have represented the closest accommodation to the station while still facing the Kent estuary. Symbolic sunflower features above the front entrance of each property are said to show that they had arranged insurance cover.

**Access**

Arnside is 4 miles south of Milnthorpe on the B5282.

# THE ALBION HOTEL'S BELL AND LIMESTONE 'BIRD'

## UNUSUAL ROOF TOP FEATURES: ONE MAN-MADE AND THE OTHER NATURAL

The Albion Hotel has a commanding roadside position at the southern end of Arnside promenade. Built in about 1810 as the home of a ship owner, Captain Robert Greenwood, ownership passed during 1854 to his son-in-law, Richard Bush, and he restyled the building to include bars and function rooms in 'Bush's Albion Hotel'.

**Access**

The Albion Hotel is at the southern end of Arnside promenade.

The bell and limestone bird on the Albion Hotel, Arnside.

Further alterations during the twentieth century have changed the building's external appearance, but a couple of unusual roof-top features have survived successive restyling schemes. A lump of limestone, mounted on the chimney, has the appearance of a sea bird but in fact it is a natural piece of limestone and has been in place for more than a century.

A large bell on the rear of the roof has also occupied its lofty position for over a hundred years. It has been suggested that it was used to give warning of the incoming tidal 'bore', but it is more likely that it was used by guests in the hotel to summon an ostler from Richard Bush's nearby coach and carriage business.

# PIEL ISLAND

## *CHEQUERED HISTORY AT AN OFFSHORE SETTING*

**Access**

Piel Island is accessible by ferry from Roa Island.

The ruined walls of Piel Castle dominate the low outline of Piel Island off Barrow-in-Furness. It dates from the early fourteenth century and was probably built as a fortified warehouse for storing cargoes away from the threat posed by raiding pirates.

Piel Island was probably a base for Celts and invading Roman forces, but the first recognised name, 'Foudray' or 'Fotheray' has Scandinavian origins and means 'fire island', which is a reference to the fire beacon used to guide boats into the channel.

From the mid-twelfth century the island prospered under Cistercian monks based at Furness Abbey on the mainland. The first wooden tower was constructed on the island and an unlimited cargo licence was granted in 1232 before the Abbey's own vessels were given royal protection in 1258.

This offshore location also proved popular with the smuggling fraternity and among the wealth of folklore that originated from these parts was the legend of the 'goose barnacle'. The basis for the story was 'feathers' and 'legs' that hung from the opening in its walls and as the barnacles were often found in the same locality as a particular type of goose, the conclusion drawn was that geese were hatched from the barnacles.

Piel Island was thrust into the national limelight in 1487 when Lambert Simnel laid claim to the English throne and led an army of German and Irish mercenaries from this offshore base on a march to London. Defeat at Stoke, just twelve days after leaving Piel Island, on 16 June saw him arrive in London as a prisoner of the king.

Following the closure of monasteries under Henry VIII, ownership of the island passed to the monarchy and Piel Castle was strengthened when the Spanish Armada posed a threat in the 1580s. During the next century a Parliamentary fleet anchored close to Piel Island after Royalists had captured Liverpool, but smuggling activities soon dominated this remote setting once again.

Piel Island off Barrow-in-Furness.

An increase in trade, notably in the iron industry, brought more shipping to Piel Island and its harbour and during the late eighteenth century a public house and properties for pilots were constructed.

The houses are now holiday homes and the inn has recently been refurbished and the landlord has the title, 'King of Piel Island'.

# FISH SLABS AND STOCKS, BROUGHTON-IN-FURNESS

## *ECHOES OF BUSY TIMES IN A MARKET CENTRE*

**Access**

Broughton-in-Furness is on the A595 about 15 miles north of Barrow-in-Furness.

Quieter times have returned to the small market town of Broughton-in-Furness on the north side of Morecambe Bay. In the centre of the main square there are clues from the days when it was a hub of activity. A weekly market catered for local produce, including fishermen's catches from the nearby River Duddon and Morecambe Bay, and the long stone fish tables are still in place beneath a huge spreading chestnut tree.

Close by are the wooden stocks where wrongdoers would be detained to face the wrath of passers by.

Stocks and fish slabs at Broughton-in-Furness.

# SEA MARK AT RAMPSIDE AND RAMPSIDE HALL

## *A LANDMARK COLUMN AND CHIMNEYS GALORE*

A tall, slender brick-built tower is prominent on the fore shore at Rampside to the south of Barrow-in-Furness, but its function is unclear. In fact it is a Victorian sea mark which was used as a 'leading light' along with similar structures at Foulney and Biggar Dyke by ships navigating a passage into Piel Channel and Barrow-in-Furness.

The two-tone brickwork is typical of Furness Railway buildings that characterised the development of Barrow as an industrial enterprise, but during the early 1990s a further phase of engineering development in the area put the sea mark's future in doubt. Following pressure from Barrow Civic Society and a review of historical buildings by English Heritage, Rampside's sea mark was given listed building status and reprieved.

Close by and across the road, Rampside Hall has a really intriguing skyline. No less than twelve chimneys spread across the roof while at a lower level many of the fourteen windows have only recently seen the light of day (after being blocked as a result of the window tax of 1696).

**Access**

The sea mark is on the foreshore at Rampside, about 3 miles south of Barrow-in-Furness via the A5087.

Sea mark at Rampside.

Sea mark at Rampside.

# SIR JOHN BARROW MONUMENT, ULVERSTON

## *A LANDMARK UNLIT LIGHTHOUSE*

**Access**

This landmark monument is within walking distance of Ulverston town centre from Hart Street or along Town Bank Road and Chittery Lane.

The Sir John Barrow Monument looks every inch of its 100ft height like a lighthouse, yet its landlocked position on Hoad Hill is about a mile from the northern edge of Morecambe Bay. Completed on 9 January 1851 and built of limestone quarried from nearby Birkrigg Common, it was designed by Andrew Trimen as a memorial to the naval administrator and traveller, Sir John Barrow, and has emblems and inscriptions linked to his distinguished career. Born in a cottage in the Dragley Beck area of Ulverston, Barrow served on a Greenland whaler before becoming a teacher at Greenwich. After learning Mandarin, he wrote a book, *Travels in China*, and then recorded journeys with Lord MaCartney to the South African heartland. Another change of direction led to him becoming Second Secretary to the Admirality where he promoted scientific surveys into the Arctic region, and in 1830 he was one of the founders of the Royal Geographic Society. During 1835 he was rewarded with a baronetcy for his achievements.

Sir John Barrow Monument on Hoad Hill, Ulverston.

A spiral staircase within the monument has 112 steps leading to a lantern chamber, which has never had a functional light even though Trinity House ruled that it should be capable of being used if occasion arose.

Plans of the structure show a basement room to accommodate the lighthouse keeper and the official position of lighthouse keeper has been maintained even though the keeper is no longer resident at the monument.

Heat damage from an adjacent beacon which had caught fire – spreading flames to Hoad Hill – during Queen Victoria's Jubilee celebrations in 1900 resulted in the outer surface receiving a coat of rendering, and further repairs costing £35,000 were carried out between 1990 and 1992.

Hoad Hill is now owned and managed by the Ulverston Town Lands Trust and the monument is opened during the summer by the lighthouse keeper and Friends of the Sir John Barrow Monument.

# MORECAMBE BAY'S TIDES

## SHIFTING SANDS, A TIDAL BORE AND THE 'QUEEN'S GUIDE'

**Access**

The Kent Channel runs southwards into Morecambe Bay between Grange-over-Sands on the west side and Silverdale and Arnside on the eastern edge.

The wide expanse of Morecambe Bay covers 120sq. miles where the Rivers Kent and Leven reach the sea to create a tidal tract of enthralling contrasts.

The narrow funnel shape of the estuary results in a small tidalwave that fronts each incoming tide. It may stand as high as a metre, though usually it is only half this height, and races across the sandy wastes at a rapid rate of up to nine knots. The rise and fall of the tide varies between 7 to 10m depending on the time of year, phases of the moon and prevailing weather conditions, and it poses an obvious and very real danger to anyone who ventures on to the sands at low tide.

For centuries travellers have crossed Morecambe Bay, but the perils of the journey have led to an inevitable loss of life. The first record of a guide is in 1501 and the current 'Queen's Guide to the Sands of Morecambe Bay', Cedric Robinson, was appointed in November 1963. Since then he has led tens of thousands of people across the sands of Morecambe Bay after checking aspects of the route during the previous day. The usual route involves crossing the channel of the River Kent and, after testing the depth and firmness of the river bed, a safe course is marked by branches of laurel.

Numerous celebrities have made the crossing and the life and work of Cedric Robinson has been featured by film and television companies from home and abroad. Perhaps the most historic crossing of the sands involved HRH the Duke of Edinburgh, who made the journey by carriage on 30 May 1985, and the most unusual must be the trek by a lady farmer from the Whitby area, who drove a flock of geese across the bay during a fundraising trip from Furness Abbey to Whitby.

Cedric Robinson and his wife, Olive, live in the Grade II listed Guide's Cottage on the west side of Grange-over-Sands and from this shoreline location he has continued cockling and shrimping activities. A lifetime of work and service in this most beautiful of natural settings has brought a deserved number of honorary degrees and awards and in 1999 he was awarded the title of MBE.

The railway viaduct across the River Kent at Arnside.

The old jetty and estuary of the River Kent at Arnside.

# THE RAVENGLASS & ESKDALE RAILWAY

## 'L'AL RATTY': MANY PEOPLE'S FAVOURITE RAILWAY

**Access**

Ravenglass is on the A595 coast road between Broughton-in-Furness and Whitehaven.

'L'al Ratty' found a place in the annals of railway history long ago. Properly named the Ravenglass & Eskdale Railway, it began in 1871 when a company called Whitehaven Iron Mines Ltd drew up plans for a 3ft gauge line from workings at Boot to link up with the Furness Railway at Ravenglass.

The railway opened for goods traffic in 1875 and a year later a licence was granted to carry passengers, but within two years the railway company was bankrupt and it was with great difficulty that the Whitehaven Iron Co. kept the line operational.

Following the failure of ironstone mining operations the line was used to carry granite and tourists, but in 1908 it was declared to be unsafe. A new company, the Eskdale Railway Co. revived the transportation of granite and iron ore, but flooding in mines at Boot finally ended operations in April 1913.

During 1915 a model railway engineer, W.J. Baseet-Lowke, came across the abandoned railway at Eskdale and after leasing it he converted the line to 15in gauge. Severe gradients meant that the line had to terminate at Dalegarth station, but goods, passengers and mail were carried all the year round.

In 1922 a local resident and industrialist, Sir Aubrey Brocklebank, opened Beckfoot granite quarry and the railway was used to transport large amounts of granite to the crushing plant at Murthwaite and then to the main line at Ravenglass.

During 1925 Henry Lithgow took over management of the railway company, but two years later the winter passenger service was withdrawn. Passenger services ended completely during the Second World War, but quarry traffic continued.

Keswick Granite Co. bought the railway in 1948, but five years later they announced that it was uneconomical and closed it down. With no offers of purchase materialising, the railway was set to be sold at auction on 7 September 1960 before a public appeal, backed by Mr Colin Gilbert and Sir Wavell Wakefield, raised the capital take over operations.

Day-to-day operations by the Railway Co. are supported by the Ravenglass & Eskdale Preservation Society with voluntary labour and publicity, and since the establishment of the company a range of improvements have been made. A new signal box has been constructed at Ravenglass, additional locomotives have been built or purchased, and station buildings have been adapted as workshops and the Ratty Arms public house.

The origins of the name 'L'al Ratty' (Little Ratty) remain unclear but the most likely explanation is that it was the nickname for the line's builder in 1874; a Mr Ratcliffe.

Ravenglass & Eskdale Railway, Ravenglass.

Carriages at Ravenglass railway station.

# RAVENGLASS ROMAN BATH HOUSE

### *ONE OF THE HIGHEST-STANDING ROMAN BUILDINGS IN THE COUNTRY*

Quieter times have returned to Ravenglass in recent years, but there is a dramatic reminder of earlier glories in the form of a Roman bath house. This shoreline location was the site of the Roman fort of Clanoventa and an important route ran from the port at Ravenglass over Hardknott Pass to the fort at Mediobogdum and through to Ambleside (Galava).

**Access**

Walls Castle, the Roman bath house, lies south-east of the village of Ravenglass and close to the former railway line.

The walls of this impressive Roman building stand 12½ft high and are said to be held together with the original mortar. Interior walls in a room by the entrance have plaster from those early days and grooves in the thresholds of two doorways may have been formed by doorframes. A smaller internal room was probably the cistern, which was connected to a furnace on the other side of the walls through a tiled flue.

Much of the history of this impressive collection of Roman rooms is based on informed speculation, but the discovery of glass below several windows clearly indicates that they were once glazed and foundations of other rooms show that they were warmed by hypocausts.

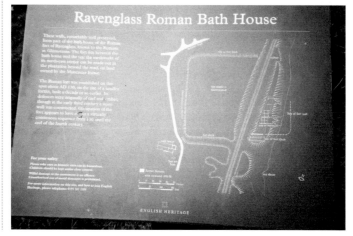

*Above:* Ravenglass Roman bath house.

*Left:* The information board at Ravenglass Roman bath house.

# ST BEES' MAN

## *A FASCINATING DISCOVERY AT THE PRIORY CHURCH OF ST MARY AND ST BEGA*

An early church of a Benedictine nunnery dating from about 650 AD was destroyed by Danish raiders and then re-established by William de Meschines in 1120. The current building, with a fine central tower and superb Norman doorway, has seen a number of additions and alterations in recent times, but the most dramatic episode associated with the church took place in 1981.

Earlier excavations had taken place in the vicinity of St Bees' Priory in the early 1950s and between 1979 and 1981, but it was the discovery of a lead coffin on 12 August 1981 that amazed archaeologists and onlookers. Excavations of an area of the church dating from around 1300 had already uncovered twelve human burials from the medieval period when archaeologists unearthed a lead coffin containing a human shaped 'parcel'.

Beeswax had been used extensively to preserve the body of a thirty-five to forty-five-year-old male within a shroud, but close examination of wounds failed to establish the cause of death. One theory maintains that injuries to his upper body may have resulted from military action or participation in a tournament. There is no indication about the identity of St Bees' Man, but speculation suggests that it could have been Anthony de Lucy, Lord of Cockermouth and Egremont, who died during an overseas campaign in 1368, or Robert of Harrington, who was buried at St Bees in 1297, but in spite of extensive DNA tests and analysis of lead from the coffin the truth about 'our brother unknown' remains a mystery.

He was reburied with due ceremony on 21 August 1981.

**Access**

St Bees is 2 miles west of Egremont on the A595 to the south of Whitehaven.

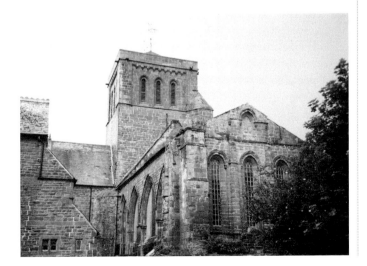

The Priory Church of St May and St Bega, St Bees.

A plaque with information about St Bees' Man at the priory.

# THE CRAB FAIR

## *EXTRAORDINARY EVENTS IN EGREMONT*

**Access**

Egremont is 5 miles south of Whitehaven on the A595.

The Crab Fair was first held at the Cumbrian coastal town of Egremont in 1267 under the terms of a royal charter granted by King Henry III. Originally the fair extended over three days, but as industrialisation reduced townspeople's leisure time, the events were confined to a single day and in recent years it has become traditional to hold the fair on the third Saturday in September.

Little is know about events of the Crab Fair until the nineteenth century, but it seems certain that blood sports such as cock fighting and bull baiting featured until they were banned by law in 1835. A typical Crab Fair in the 1800s began at dawn with the installation of the greasy pole 'at the fish stone by the Market Cross.' The pole measured 30ft in height and was greased with lard. Contestants attempted to climb to the top in order to retrieve the prize, which was usually a hat (probably a top hat) and the winner then paraded around town sporting his new headpiece. In 1852 the prize became a side of

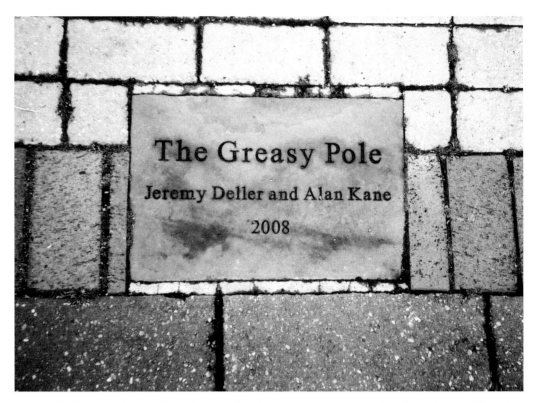

An inscribed stone at the site of the Greasy Pole in Egremont, commemorating the designers of the pole.

mutton and if it was not won by the end of the day, then it was cut up and distributed to poor folk. This tradition continues to the present day and in addition to the main prize, ribbons are now attached to the pole which can be grasped and exchanged for gifts in the town.

Events continued with a cattle market and in the afternoon a range of sporting events got underway. Midday was the signal for the 'scattering of apples,' now known as the Parade of the Apple Cart, which probably originates from a celebration of the end of the harvest. Cumberland wrestling features prominently and other amusements include a pipe-smoking contest (to determine the fastest person to smoke a clay pipe of tobacco), horn blowing and the world-famous gurning championships.

Gurning is pulling an ugly face through a braffin (horse collar). Competitors are not allowed to use their hands or artificial aids (although they may remove their false teeth) and they thrash around the stage while the braffin is held by the referee. The winner is the person with the most altered face.

Gurning is said to have begun when a farm worker took a bite of a local crab apple and, because of its extremely sour taste, pulled an ugly face (or a gurn). A bystander put a collar around him and the competition was born.

The Greasy Pole, Egremont.

A painting of Anne Woods, Ladies Gurning Champion.

Tommy Mattinson, current World Gurning Champion.

# five

# Southern Lakes (Inland)

# GOLDEN RULE INN, AMBLESIDE

## *THE MEANING BEHIND THE NAME AND AN OUTSIZE FISHY CATCH*

**Access**

The Golden Rule public house is close to the centre of Ambleside.

Most pub names have a fascinating story to divulge and this is certainly true of the Golden Rule near the centre of Ambleside. Although there were many taverns with this name about 150 years ago, there are now only two left in England. Apart from this one in Ambleside, the other is at Dagnall in Buckinghamshire (and a recently opened venue in Fountainbridge, Edinburgh, which was formerly known as the Yeoman Bar).

The reason for the unusual name is that public houses were not only prohibited from selling wines and spirits, but also the golden rule of not opening their doors on a Sunday was being applied. This arrangement ensured that agricultural and other local workers remained sober and in an appropriate frame of mind for attending church services.

During the industrial revolution many workers moved to town-based occupations where public houses were open on Sundays, which in turn led to an increasing demand for rural hostelries to follow suit. In time, all but two changed their names.

The Golden Rule Inn, Ambleside.

An over-sized fish on display in the Golden Rule Inn.

Another suggestion is that the name is linked to the Biblical quote and a golden rule of life: 'Do unto others as you would have them do unto you.'

On one of the Golden Rule's inside walls there is a genuine curiosity in the form of a fish mounted in a display case with its head and tail sticking out of each end. A brass plaque on the wooden frame states, 'Stuffed and mounted by John Hargreaves 1992.'

# BRIDGE HOUSE, AMBLESIDE

## *TINY PROPERTY WITH A WATERY PROSPECT*

With just one bay for width and another for depth, this tiny property sits on a bridge over the Stock Beck and must rank as a contender for the smallest house in England.

One tale states that it was built by a Scottish family who were attempting to avoid payment of ground rent, but the truth is that it was built in 1723 by the Braithwaite family as a crossing point over the beck between Ambleside Hall and their orchard (before the road was re-routed).

At one time apples were stored in the upper room and after the hall was sold a number of tradesmen used these most unusual premises, but eventually Bridge House fell into disrepair. Local folk had such a high regard for this curious little building that they raised £450 to pay for repairs and then in 1928 handed it over to the National Trust, who are still based there.

**Access**

Ambleside is on the A591 at the head of Lake Windermere.

Bridge House, Ambleside.                              Irton Cross.

# IRTON CROSS

## *A MAGNIFICENT EXAMPLE OF SAXON STONEWORK*

**Access**

St Paul's
Church, Irton,
is signposted
from the
A595 heading
north from
Ravenglass.

There are superb views of mountain peaks from Irton's spreading churchyard, but it is the man-made beauty of a Saxon cross that takes the eye. Measuring 10ft in height, this slender sandstone column tapers gently to a fine head piece. Its edges still have vine scrolls and on the face and back there are swirly-patterned rosettes with Irish origins. This splendid example of ninth-century craftsmanship is positioned close to the centre of the churchyard around St Paul's Church and in terms of beauty and state of preservation it ranks close to the Gosforth Cross.

# HARDKNOTT FORT

## *A LINK IN THE LINE OF ROMAN DEFENCES*

The Roman fort of Medibogdum has a commanding position above the road from Ravenglass to Ambleside and is regarded as one of the finest examples in Britain. From this spur projecting from the south-west side of the mountain of Hardknott, between the valleys of Eskdale and Hardknott Gill, there are views of Scafell Pikes less than 4 miles away.

A line of defensive forts was constructed during the governorship of Agricola and about 500 soldiers were based here between 90 and 190 AD. It is almost square with gates in the centre of each wall. The internal area covers about 3 acres and includes the excavated sites of the commander's house, a pair of granaries and an administration block.

External walls are 6ft thick and on the south side is a small bath block with a sequence of three rooms offering cold, warm and hot treatment. An additional detached circular hot bath is located nearby. On the north-east side of the fort lies a levelled area covering 3 acres which is linked to the fort. It is believed to have served as a parade ground.

This splendid site is managed by the National Trust and English Heritage. Interpretative boards help to explain the layout and operations of the fort.

[It is worth noting that Hardknott Pass is probably the most daunting of all the Lakeland passes. A gradient of 1 in 4 coupled with hairpin bends offers a severe challenge to even the most experienced of drivers.]

**Access**

Hardknott Roman Fort is 9 miles north-east of Ravenglass at the west end of Hardknott Pass.

Hardknott Roman fort.

Hardknott Roman fort.

# HORSE TROUGH AT HAWKSHEAD

## AN IMPRESSIVE ROADSIDE DRINKING STATION

**Access**

Heading
northwards
from
Hawkshead
on the B5285,
then the first
left turn and
after about
2 miles the
trough is on the
left as the hill
runs down to
Coniston.

Roadside drinking places take many different shapes and forms, but few are quite as grand as the imposing structure on the road from Hawkshead to Coniston.

A solid central stone tower is flanked by two slightly lower square towers with a horse trough on one side and a simple seat for travellers on the other. The middle block has a drinking station for humans, with the words, 'Keep the pavement dry' engraved on the cast-iron panel above the manufacturer's name 'T. Kennedy, Patentee, Kilmarnock.'

This impressive watering place was erected in 1885 by Susanna Beever and an engraving on a stone slab offers advice for horse rides by stating:

A Righteous Man
Regards the life
of his Beast

The horse trough and seat at Hawkshead.

IN MEMORIAM. ERECTED BY SUSANNA BEEVER 1885.

The inscription on the horse trough at Hawkshead.

HE SENDETH THE SPRINGS INTO THE RIVERS WHICH RUN AMONG THE HILLS

The inscription on the horse trough at Hawkshead.

# GRIZEDALE FOREST SCULPTURES

## AN AMAZING ARRAY OF SCULPTED TIMBER PIECES

**Access**

Situated
between Lake
Coniston and
Windermere,
Grizedale
Forest is
signposted
to the left
just before
Hawkshead.

The Sculpture Project was set up in 1977 'to provide a working environment for sculptors … to create projects which vitally spring from their response to the forest.' More than thirty years later the sculptures in Grizedale Forest have blended into the natural background, but they still offer an unexpected and sometimes startling spectacle during a stroll along way marked trails.

A wide range of carvings include sheep and birds in tree branches as well as a life-sized figure called 'Ancient Forester' and a tree hung with dozens of simple wooden chairs. Grizedale Forest was also noted for its 'Theatre in the Forest', which drew international performers and musicians, while swing and zip slides offered an exhilarating alternative for those of an adventurous nature. Although this event has not taken place in recent years, Grizedale Forest still provides an extraordinary outdoor experience.

Grizedale Forest sculptures.

*Right & below:* Grizedale Forest sculptures.

# GREATEST LIAR IN THE WORLD COMPETITION

**Access**

Santon Bridge
is between
Eskdale Green
and Gosforth
on the east side
of the A595.

## TELLING THE TALLEST OF TALL STORIES

The clear waters of the River Irt race over a rocky bed before passing under an attractive stone arch at Santon Bridge, where the nearby inn is the venue for one of this country's most improbable competitions. An enchanting setting in Wasdale is the unlikely location for the Greatest Liar in the World contest.

This highly unusual tournament is held in honour of Will Ritson, born in 1808, and landlord of the Wasdale Head Inn who triumphed in the original contest and Ritson's Bar at his inn is named after him. Every year entrants converge on Santon Bridge from all over the country, but one of the rules of this incredible verbal encounter states that alleged professional liars such as journalists, politicians and lawyers are not allowed to enter.

*Above:* Bridge Inn at Santon Bridge, the setting for the Greatest Liar in the World competition.

*Left:* The tablet on the wall of the Bridge Inn, Santon Bridge.

# ST OLAF'S CHURCH, WASDALE HEAD

## *SEVERAL OF ENGLAND'S HIGHEST MOUNTAINS*

The little village of Wasdale Head is encircled by several of England's mountains including Great Gable and the Scafells, with narrow, walled lanes threading through to the grey stone houses. A little distance away, screened by yew trees, is the tiny church of St Olaf.

Measuring only 40ft in length and 17ft wide, it lays claim to being one of the smallest churches in the country. Much of the building dates from the sixteenth century and the roof is said to be constructed from ship timbers. Three windows admit light to an interior that has trim oak seats with bobbin ends and an old piscina in the tiny chancel. The churchwarden's staves are said to be unique with a ram's head depicted on one and a ewe's head on the other.

The church's close bond with the surrounding peaks is emphasised by many of the burials in the adjacent churchyard. Climbers were drawn to this location in the late nineteenth century and the Fell and Rock Climbing Club of the English Lake District was formed, but down the years the forbidding slopes have claimed many victims. One particularly poignant grave marks the final resting place of four young men who died through a fall, when roped together, from Pinnacle Rock on Scafell in 1903.

The attractive Napes Needle window has the quotation, 'I will lift up mine eyes unto the hills from whence cometh my strength,' and represents a fitting memorial to members of the Fell and Rock Climbing Club who died in the First World War.

**Access**

Wasdale Head is 5 miles west of Gosforth (on the A595) on the north side of Wast Water.

St Olaf's Church, Wasdale Head.

The interior
of St Olaf's
Church.

# STEAM YACHT *GONDOLA*

## *STYLISH TRAVEL IN VICTORIAN ELEGANCE*

**Access**

*Gondola's* jetty
at Coniston
Pier is located
at the end of
Lake Road.
Coniston is
on the A593
between
Broughton-in-
Furness and
Ambleside.

Coniston Water lies outside the main tourist areas of the Lakes and its tranquil
setting is ideally suited to that most sedate form of travel – by Venetian-style
gondola.

The steam yacht *Gondola* was commissioned by Sir James Ramsden, general
manager of the Furness Railway Co., during the 1850s and cost 1,000 guineas.
Launched in 1859 on Coniston Water, she first carried passengers during the
following year in saloons offering first-class luxury surroundings, or a rather
more basic third-class setting.

After seventy-six years of service *Gondola* was taken out of service, although
her sister steamer, *The Lady of the Lake*, operated for three more years.

After the war, in 1945, *Gondola* was brought back into use as a houseboat, but
during the 1960s she was beached in stormy weather and became derelict. In
an attempt to save the vessel from the breaker's yard, she was deliberately sunk
in an excavated channel to preserve her iron plates. During the mid-1970s a
group of National Trust supporters decided to save this fine Victorian boat
and *Gondola* was completely rebuilt by Vickers Shipbuilding. In 1980 she was
re-launched on Coniston Water and has continued to ferry passengers to John
Ruskin's home, 'Brantwood.'

Ruskin is believed to have travelled on *Gondola* during his time at 'Brantwood'
from 1872 up to his death in 1900. No doubt he was inspired in his work as an
artist, economist and conservationist by the magnificent scenery that surrounds
Cumbria's third largest lake with gentle meadows and wooded hills ringed by
distant mountains dominated by the 2,635 ft Old Man of Coniston.

Steam yacht *Gondola* with 'Brantwood' in the background.

Steam yacht *Gondola* on Coniston Water.

# DRUNKEN DUCK INN, NEAR HAWKSHEAD

## *OUR INEBRIATED FEATHERED FRIENDS*

Down the years this country's inns and taverns have given rise to a number of unlikely or improbable tales and more often than not they are spiced with a humorous tone.

At the Drunken Duck Inn, just outside Hawkshead, the story is that beer seeped out of the cellar and into the ducks' feeding trough. The landlady

**Access**

The Drunken Duck Inn is a mile north-west of Outgate on the B5286 between Hawkshead and Ambleside.

The weather vane at the Drunken Duck Inn, near Hawkshead.

The Drunken Duck Inn.

found the birds lying about looking lifeless. Thinking they were dead, she began to pluck them for dinner.

Before long the ducks started to sober up and gained a reprieve. The landlady could do nothing for their befuddled state, but she could make up for the lost feathers and, according to this implausible story, the plucked ones were eventually returned to their pens wearing little knitted jumpers.

# HAWKSHEAD GRAMMAR SCHOOL AND ST MICHAEL'S AND ALL ANGELS,' HAWKSHEAD

## *LINKS WITH WILLIAM WORDSWORTH AND UNUSUAL CHURCH ITEMS*

There are links with William Wordsworth throughout the Lake District, but some of the strangest ties are to be found in Hawkshead. It was here, at Hawkshead Grammar School, that he received an early education during which time he carved his name into a desk top. The inscription is still on view underneath a small glass covering.

The school was founded in 1585 by Archbishop Edwin Sandys and 100 pupils could be educated in this small building. Sentences are written on the walls of the main room and the one in front of Wordsworth's desk reads, 'Books, we know are a substantial world both pure and good.'

Overlooking William Wordsworth's old school is St Michael and All Angels' Church, which has a number of exhibits linked to earlier church practices. A pitch-pipe with ten notes was used in the church until 1828 to give the keynote of psalms, and wooden staves with yellow-painted knobs were carried either by churchwardens or stewards.

The chest was produced in response to an ecclesiastical ruling of 1603 which stated that the safekeeping of the parish register book should be ensured by fitting a solid chest with locks, the key of which would be held by the minister and two churchwardens. A massive oak beam measuring 6ft 8in in length was used to fashion the cavity which was just 3ft long. The bands are also of oak.

A similar, smaller chest in the church was fashioned from a cambered or thickened portion of one of the old tie beams that were removed when the clerestory was added. The cavity would be hollowed out by broadening the mortice hole for the foot of the king post.

Near the vestry door hangs a 'Buried in Woolen affidavit' which originated from some strange legislation in the 1660s. In 1666 Parliament determined that all burials must be in cloth or clothing made wholly from wool, but this attempt to reduce the import of linen was largely ignored until further legislation was introduced in 1669. It stated that within eight days of any burial an affidavit had to be prepared showing that the corpse had indeed been interred in 'Woolen only.'

Almost 200 of these affidavits, or certificates, linked to burials in 1680 and 1696 have been preserved in the church.

**Access**

Hawkshead Grammar School and the parish church are in the centre of Hawkshead which is 3 miles east of Coniston (between Coniston Water and Windermere).

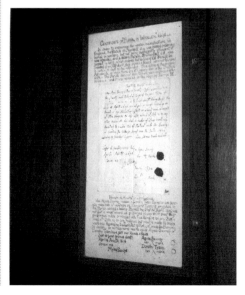

*Above top:* St Michael and All Angels' Church.

*Above:* The parish chest at St Michael and All Angels'.

*Left:* Affidavit in St Michael and All Angels' Church.

# AA BOX NEAR GRASMERE

## *A RARE BEACON OF HOPE FOR STRANDED MOTORISTS*

For more than ninety years motorists had the re-assuring sight of roadside boxes sporting the letters 'AA' on their side, and in more remote rural areas they stood out like a bright beacon of hope for stranded motorists. Sadly, however, the old adage again proved to be true and all good things must come to an end.

In September 2002 the Automobile Association announced that it was phasing out most of its 552 roadside phones because of lack of use. The first AA sentry box was installed in Ashstead, Surrey, in 1911 and early boxes were initially intended to be used as shelters for passing patrols. Before long they were made available to members who could telephone for assistance, free of charge, if their car had broken down. Early boxes were even equipped with fire extinguishers and in 1920 keys were issued to members to allow access.

**Access**

AA Box 487 is just north of Grasmere on the A591 climbing towards Dunmail Rise.

Design features changed over the years and in 1925 'superboxes' began to appear at major road junctions, complete with illuminated direction signs on top. However, by the 1970s the old style boxes began to be phased out – apart from those that had been given listed status – in favour of the free-standing pedestal phones.

The distinctive yellow panels on the boxes show the family's livery colour of the 5th Earl of Lonsdale and Lowther (in Cumbria). He originated the well-known boxing belt and was president of the Automobile Association in 1907.

By the early years of the new millennium the AA were receiving around 5½ million calls, but fewer than 6,000 came from the boxes with the vast majority of motorists making use of their mobile phones.

Among the few remaining examples of an old AA box is the little black and yellow sentry post on the A591, to the north of Grasmere. With a backdrop of rolling Lakeland fells, Box 487 seems to be taking pride in its status as a listed building of architectural and historic interest.

The AA box at Dunmail Rise, Grasmere.

# STORRS TEMPLE

## *CURIOUS REMINDER OF GRAND LAKELAND OCCASIONS*

**Access**

Storrs Temple
extends from
the shoreline
close to Storrs
Hall on the
south side of
Bowness on
Windermere
(beside the
A592).

Storrs Hall has a majestic position on the shore of Lake Windermere with commanding views of bays, islands and distant fells. The core of the house was built during the 1790s by Sir John Legard, to designs by the architect Joseph Gandy, who enlarged and extended the property under the ownership of John Bolton between 1808–11.

During Bolton's time at Storrs Hall the spacious grounds, reception rooms and adjacent lake were the setting for gatherings of intellectuals and wits of the day who would take part in morning cavalcades through the woodland, moonlight boating on the lake and large-scale regattas.

Typical of these impressive gatherings was the celebration of Sir Walter Scott's birthday in 1825 when guests including William Wordsworth, Robert Southey, John Wilson and George Canning attended a regatta which started form Storrs Point, south of Bowness. It is likely that spectators watched proceedings form Storrs Temple, an octagonal building which stands at the end of a jetty from shores close to the hall. Known locally as 'the Fishing House' it has four arches and four tablets with inscriptions honouring the achievements of four admirals of the fleet, Duncan, St Vincent, Nelson and Howe.

This curious monument was part of Gandy's scheme in 1804 and still makes an ideal vantage point for taking in dramatic Lakeland scenery.

Storrs Hall, Windermere.

Temple at Storrs Hall.

A view through a window of the temple.

# CALGARTH ... AND THE STEAM LAUNCH *DOLLY*

## *FLYING BOATS AND THE WORLD'S OLDEST MECHANICALLY PROPELLED STEAMBOAT STILL IN WORKING ORDER*

The wartime years 1939–45 brought major changes to aspects of industry, but one of the most unlikely developments saw the quiet waters of Lake Windermere play a major role in this country's aviation industry.

Short Brothers Ltd was established by Eustace, Oswald and Horace Short in 1908 and soon became Britain's foremost aircraft manufacturer. During 1915 a Seaplane Works was set up on the River Medway at Rochester, in Kent, and in 1937 the Sunderland flying boat was manufactured alongside the Empire passenger-carrying flying boats. Wartime service saw the Sunderlands used in the North Atlantic Campaign to escort convoys of merchant vessels and to track down German U-boats.

By 1940 German bombers were attacking areas of Kent, including Rochester, and the decision was made by the Ministry of Aircraft Production

**Access**

Calgarth and the Steamboat Museum are on the north side of Windermere close to Troutbeck Bridge.

to move some of the manufacturing of the Sunderland to a safer location. These aircraft needed a large expanse of water for take-off and because of its comparatively remote location, White Cross Bay on Windermere was chosen as the setting for a factory.

When part of Short Brothers' skilled workforce moved to the newly completed factory at Windermere, they were initially housed in local lodgings, but during 1941 construction work got underway on a sector of land at Troutbeck Bridge.

Accommodation was provided for 200 married couples and separate hostels could house 300 single workers. By the end of 1942 this new community of Calgarth also included a primary school, two shops, a canteen, assembly hall, club house, laundry, sick bay, policeman and football team. Workers had arrived from many parts of the country and their homes were affectionately termed 'Shorts' Palaces,' but local folk evidently referred to this new community as 'China town.'

Windermere's shoreline waters hold another tantalising clue to this area's part in wartime aviation in the form of underwater metal rails for launching Short's flying boats.

Among the items housed in the Windermere Steamboat Museum is the world's oldest mechanically propelled boat still in working order.

In 1851 the steam launch *Dolly* began service on Windermere as one of the lake's first pleasure craft and after well over forty years of service she was sold in 1894 for service on Ullswater. Sadly, the following year brought freezing

A view towards Calgarth on Windermere, where Sunderland flying boats were manufactured.

conditions and *Dolly* was trapped in the ice. Water seeped into the boat causing her to sink to a depth of 45ft, where she stayed until 1960. Much of the vessel was covered in silt when teams of divers located and then examined *Dolly*, but, with an appreciation of her importance to steam boating, plans were made to salvage and restore this amazing craft.

On 8 November 1962, *Dolly* was lifted from the bottom of the lake then towed to Glenridding pier for a thorough cleaning.

Some seventy years after leaving Windermere, *Dolly* was moved back over the Kirkstone Pass and back to the slipway at Calgarth Park. From there this incredible vessel was towed to Rayrigg Hall for a thorough investigation and it was then decided to carry out a full restoration of the boiler and engine.

Once this was completed, engines were started and *Dolly* moved out across the waters of Windermere. The original boiler continued in use for ten years and she is now on display at the Windermere Steamboat Museum.

# THE MORTAL MAN

## *TIMELY GUIDANCE FOR THE HUMAN RACE AT A RURAL INN*

Located in the depths of the Troutbeck Valley, amid landscapes that have inspired poets, painters and authors, is another of Cumbria's hostelries with an unusual name.

**Access**

The Mortal Man is situated between Kirkstone and Windermere at the base of Troutbeck Valley.

The Mortal Man Inn, Troutbeck.

The weather vane on the Mortal Man Inn.

The sign for the Mortal Man Inn.

Built in 1689 by Isaac Cookson as a small ale house for this remote neighbourhood, the Mortal Man Inn probably derives its name from four lines of salutary advice which were displayed on the outside sign:

O, mortal man, that lives by bread,
What is it makes thy nose so red?
Thou silly fool, that look'st so pale,
'Tis drinking Sally Birkett's ale.

# CASTLE HOUSE OBELISK

## *A MASSIVE MONUMENT IN CELEBRATION OF FREEDOM*

**Access**

Castle Howe is on the south side of the township close to the Town Hall.

Set in the lowland valley of the River Kent, Kendal has prospered since Roman times as a market centre and its layout is characterised by narrow lanes or yards branching off the main streets at right angles. Opposite the Town Hall a roadway runs uphill to Castle Howe, which marks the site of a motte and bailey castle. It was built soon after 1092 as the border was pushed northwards, but as the medieval township of Kendal spread northwards beyond Kirkland, a new castle was built of stone between 1220 and 1280. The abandoned bailey

Castle Howe Obelisk, Kendal.

An inscribed tablet on Castle Howe Obelisk.

on Castle Howe later became known as 'Bowling Fell' when it was used for bowling greens.

The summit of the grassy mound is dominated by an obelisk which was erected in 1788 to celebrate the Glorious Revolution 100 years earlier, when William of Orange replaced James II as monarch. It displays the slogan 'Sacred to Liberty.' To the Kendal Whigs who subscribed to the fund for erecting the obelisk this meant social justice, electoral freedom and abolition of tithes. The obelisk was constructed by William Holme using designs by Francis Webster. Francis and his son, George, were Kendal's foremost architects for the next forty years.

# KENDAL TOWN HALL CARILLON

## *MUSICAL INTERLUDES IN THE TOWN CENTRE*

**Access**

Kendal Town Hall is in the town centre at the junction of Lowther Street and Stricklandgate.

The old Assembly Rooms at Kendal date from 1825–7, but in the early 1890s the purchase of adjacent properties allowed major alterations to be carried out. Ionic columns and a tower with a French-style pavilion cap were incorporated into the new Town Hall building and some of the cost was met by a bequest from Alderman William Bindloss of Castle Green. He provided £6,000 towards building costs and a further £3,000 for the new carillon of bells in the restyled tower.

The new clock and its carillon (set of bells for playing tunes) were set in motion at 11 a.m. on 22 June 1897 as part of Queen Victoria's Diamond Jubilee celebrations. A different set of tunes from England, Ireland, Scotland and Wales is featured each day starting at 6 a.m. and repeated at intervals of three hours through to midnight. They are:

Sunday:        Devotion
Monday:        Kelvin Grove
Tuesday:       British Grenadiers
Wednesday:     All Through the Night
Thursday:      When the King Enjoys His Own Again
Friday:        Garry Owen
Saturday:      There's Nae Luck Aboot the House

The Town Hall, Kendal.

Carillon on Kendal Town Hall.

# THE LEYLAND MOTORS' CLOCK

## *A QUIETER LOCATION FOR THIS IMPRESSIVE TIMEPIECE*

A ground-level setting in front of the Brewery Arts Centre is the unlikely location for an impressive timepiece like the Leyland Motors' Clock, but an adjacent panel gives the following explanation:

**Access**

Leyland Motors' Clock is positioned in front of the Brewery Arts Centre close to Highgate.

> This clock was originally located on the A6 road near Shap Fell. It was one of seven clocks that were erected at prominent locations on major trunk roads in 1931 by Leyland Motors Limited.
>
> The clock was relocated to this site in 1973 and refurbished in 1996 by enthusiasts as part of the celebrations to mark 100 years of British Commercial Vehicle manufacture.
>
> This stone donated by The Shap Memorial Trust.

Leyland Motors' Clock, Kendal.

An inscribed stone at the base of the Leyland Motors' Clock.

# THE SNUFF FACTORY

## SCENT OF AN EARLIER TRADING COMMODITY

**Access**

The snuff factory is at No. 27 Lowther Street off Highgate.

Kendal's lanes and side roads have plenty of interesting features including an effigy of a pipe-smoking Turk in Lowther Street. This colourful Eastern character is mounted halfway up the wall of No. 27 and certainly brightens this rather gloomy side road.

This carving is a replica of one which was displayed here from 1870 and represents a typical snuff house trading sign. It is thought that it was copied from the Turks Head coffee house in London, which was visited by Samuel Johnson and his associates.

Kendal's close proximity to the port of Whitehaven enabled the town's traders to export cotton and import tobacco. Lettering on the brickwork – 'Tobacco and Snuff Manufacturers' – serves as a reminder of the days when Kendal had a thriving tobacco industry and Samuel Gawith (Gawith, Hoggarth & Co.), makers of Kendal snuff since 1792, still have their offices in the Canal Head area of the town.

Snuff factory at Kendal.

A pipe-smoking Turk on the wall of the snuff factory in Lowther Street.

# THE BLACK HOG OF STRICKLANDGATE

## *BRISTLING LINK WITH AN EARLIER BUSINESS*

In the days before shop fronts were covered by lettering and coloured signs, traders displayed symbols of their trade at upper levels to attract passing custom. Perhaps the best known was the barber's stripey candy stick, but on Stricklandgate close to the centre of Kendal it is a bristly hog that catches the eye.

This impressive feature now looks rather out of place on the walls of an estate agency, but it provides an interesting link with earlier days when Kendal had a thriving brush-making industry.

**Access**

The black hog sign is at first-floor level on Stricklandgate in the centre of Kendal.

Black hog on a property in Stricklandgate.

A plaque on the wall of Black Hall in Stricklandgate, Kendal.

**BLACK HALL**

Kendal's first Alderman lived here in 1575. The house was modernised in 1810 and in 1869 became a brush factory with the sign of a bristly hog.

**KENDAL CIVIC SOCIETY**

Black hog in Stricklandgate, serving as a reminder of the brush-making industry.

# MILES THOMPSON

**Access**

Beast Banks is on the west side of Kendal, reached via Allhallows Lane from Highgate.

A monument to Miles Thompson on No. 21 Beast Banks at Kendal.

## ROOF-TOP REMINDER OF A LOCAL DESIGNER

Memorials to notable local characters take many different forms and often it is the simplest of monuments that really catch the eye. There is probably no better way to mark the design work of local architect, Miles Thompson, than to depict him gazing across the township where he designed so many public and domestic buildings.

A plaque by Kendal Civic Society on the wall of No. 21 Beast Banks gives details of Miles Thompson's life and work in the town and explains the origins of this gable-end statue.

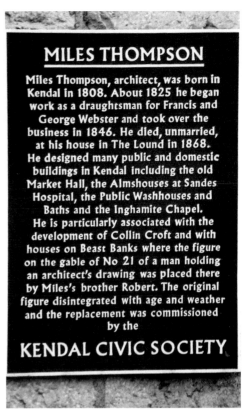

**MILES THOMPSON**

Miles Thompson, architect, was born in Kendal in 1808. About 1825 he began work as a draughtsman for Francis and George Webster and took over the business in 1846. He died, unmarried, at his house in The Lound in 1868. He designed many public and domestic buildings in Kendal including the old Market Hall, the Almshouses at Sandes Hospital, the Public Washhouses and Baths and the Inghamite Chapel. He is particularly associated with the development of Collin Croft and with houses on Beast Banks where the figure on the gable of No 21 of a man holding an architect's drawing was placed there by Miles's brother Robert. The original figure disintegrated with age and weather and the replacement was commissioned by the

**KENDAL CIVIC SOCIETY**

Statue of Miles Thompson on the roof-top.

A plaque about Miles Thompson at Beast Banks.

# KENDAL CASTLE AND A TINY BOOK

## *CATHERINE PARR CONNECTIONS*

**Access**

Kendal Castle is close to the A591 or junction 37 from the M6 motorway. The mayor's parlour is located in the centre of town.

The ruins of Kendal Castle spread along a hilltop overlooking the town and Kent valley where Roman legions previously had a base. Dating from the twelfth century, a deep ditch surrounds thick perimeter walls, with fragments of domestic buildings and three towers.

Ownership of the castle passed through the de Brus, Roos and Parr families, and the last wife of Henry VIII was born here in 1510. She was the daughter of Sir Thomas Parr, who became controller of the king's household, but died when Catherine was aged five. Her mother ensured that Catherine received a fine education, particularly in foreign languages, and after two previous

Kendal Castle is situated on a ridge above the River Kendal.

marriages she was thirty-one when she married Henry (becoming his sixth and final wife). Catherine Parr's academic upbringing enabled her to play a major role in educating their children, who grew up to be Edward VI, Queen Mary and Queen Elizabeth I, and one of the books that she used as a tutor is still on display in the town.

This tiny book is bound in silver and measures just 2½in by 1½in. A few years ago it was discovered at an antique dealer's premises in London, marked for sale at £500 and probably destined for an American collection, when a Kendal resident realised its historic value. The corporation in Kendal formed a committee to raise a fund for buying it and this fascinating Tudor work was returned to the town (where it is still on display, by arrangement with the town council, in the mayor's parlour).

# HOLY TRINITY CHURCH, KENDAL

## *MAJESTIC DIMENSIONS OF A LOFTY TOWER AND SPRAWLING AISLES*

**Access**

Holy Trinity Church is at the southern end of Kendal between the A591 and the River Kent.

Most churches have a number of outstanding features and unusual stories that help to create a truly unique atmosphere, but in some cases it is the dimensions of the building that single out a place of worship for special notice.

Kendal's Holy Trinity Church is unusual because of its overall size, where four aisles are included within the nave and chancel in a similar form to the Church of St Lateran in Rome. These sets of double aisles give an exceptional width that is balanced by a square tower which stands around 80ft high and house ten bells.

Holy Trinity Church, Kendal.

Both the exterior and interior of this spreading church were drastically altered between 1850–2, but it retains the splendid outlook towards the River Kent.

The beautiful Bellingham Chapel has original bosses on its roof and a number of links with the Bellingham family. A helmet lodged in the chapel gave rise to a curious story which found its way into Sir Walter Scott's epic poem 'Rokeby'. Set during the English Civil War, the episode involved Major Robert Phillipson, who lived on Belle Isle in Lake Windermere. Following a quarrel with a Cromwellian officer, he is said to have charged into the church while a service was taking place only for the helmet to be knocked off his head and kept as a memorial to his insolence.

Sir Walter Scott used the tale to describe how Bertram Risingham rode into the church at Rokeby, shot Oswald, and was then himself killed in the nave.

**HOLY TRINITY**

The earliest parts of this church are 13th century although an earlier church is recorded by the Domesday Survey of 1086. Most of the fabric was built about 1400–1600 when the town's cloth trade was at its peak. In 1553 Queen Mary gave the living to Trinity College, Cambridge, which is still its patron. The church is the largest in Cumbria and in the 19th century regularly accommodated about 1100 people.

KENDAL CIVIC SOCIETY

A plaque at Holy Trinity Church.

# ROMAN MILESTONE AT MIDDLETON

## *A SOLITARY COLUMN IN A FARMER'S FIELD*

It is not unusual for outdoor enthusiasts to come across single stone columns in fields or rolling expanses of countryside. Usually they are the sole survivor

**Access**

The milestone is prominent in a field overlooking the church between Kirkby Lonsdale and Scdbcrgh on the A683.

from a pair of gateposts or a simple memorial to a local individual, but the 4ft high column in a field close to Middleton Church has stood there for almost 2,000 years.

Roman legions arrived on England's southern shores in AD 43 and by AD 78 a whole network of routes had spread northwards through this country and into the lowlands of Scotland. The Middleton Milestone marks a point on the roadway between Ribchester and Carlisle at a time when troops could be required to move rapidly over the Empire's northern frontier to deal with warlike tribes.

A Roman milestone at Middleton.

# BONNIE PRINCE CHARLIE'S CHIMNEY

## *A POSSIBLE ROYAL HIDEAWAY*

The back lanes and quiet corners of some of our towns and villages can often reveal interesting facets of earlier history. Many of these features are wrapped in local folklore or hearsay which can lead to any amount of speculation and debate.

An alleyway in Sedbergh leads from the main street to Weaver's Yard, where a tall stone-built property has a broad chimney in which Bonnie Prince Charlie is said to have

Bonnie Prince Charlie's Chimney, Sedbergh.

taken refuge. Charles Edward Stuart came south from Scotland in an attempt to capture the English throne, but following defeat in battle on Clifton Moor, south of Penrith, he was forced to flee, disguised as a woman. His destination was the Isle of Skye and on the way he undoubtedly took refuge with supporters.

The chimney is wide enough to 'roast an ox' and could easily shelter a man but, on the other hand, so could many other nooks and crannies in the neighbourhood.

**Access**

Weaver's Yard is close to the town centre in Sedbergh (which is on the A684, east of Kendal and towards Hawes).

# CANNON HOUSE, SEDBERGH

## *UPWARD FACING ORDNANCE PIECES*

Cannon House overlooks Sedbergh School playing fields and in addition to the usual external features there are two small cannons set into tarmac surrounding the building. Pointing skywards, these curious iron ordnances have escaped the scrap merchant's yard and are said to date from the Jacobite Rebellion of 1745, when the house was said to have been used by fleeing rebel forces.

Time and again the truth blurs into folklore, but at least these redundant artillery pieces proved yet another talking point.

**Access**

Cannon House is situated in the centre of Sedbergh, overlooking the school playing fields.

Cannon House, Sedbergh.

Upturned cannon at Cannon House, Sedbergh.

# THE SEDBERGH SYNCHRONOME

## *A TRULY AMAZING TIMEPIECE*

**Access**

The Tourist
Information
Centre is
located in
Main Street
at Sedbergh,
which is on the
A684 between
Kendal and
Hawes.

In the current age of digital technology there are numerous highly innovative and unusual timepieces to be found, but few, if any, can hold greater interest than Frank Hope Jones' Synchronome. It consists of a pendulum clock with an electrically driven gravity escapement, which controls a number of separate dials.

Frank Hope Jones (1868–1950) was a horologist and wireless enthusiast from a family with a whole range of scientific skills. He invented the Synchronome in 1895 and established the Synchronome Co. Ltd at Nos 32 and 34 Clerkenwell Road, London, to manufacture it.

During 1921 Frank Hope Jones collaborated with W. Hamilton Shortt to produce a clock with unparalleled accuracy of timekeeping. (They were accurate to about one second a year.) About 100 Shortt Clocks were manufactured for astronomical observatories all over the world, with the first at Edinburgh in 1921, and Shortt Clocks were used at the Royal Greenwich Observatory from 1921 until 1942, when they were replaced by quartz crystal clocks.

A photograph from 1935 shows Albert Epstein and Frank Hope Jones after the successful use of a Shortt Clock to measure the time in an experiment on relativity.

Synchronome No. 526 was given to Sedbergh School by F.G. (Bobby) Woodhouse, who taught at the school from 1897 to 1930, in January 1930, and it has been running ever since. It was moved from it original position near the Bursar's Office to the Physics Laboratory and there are five dials around the school. There was also a mechanism to ring the school bells at regular intervals, but this was removed by school authorities some time ago.

Bobby Woodhouse also had a Synchronome at his house, No. 2 Highfield Villas, and on his death in 1957 it was left to the people of Sedbergh and installed in Sedbergh Rural District Council offices in Bainbridge Road. The clock was removed to Kendal by the newly established South Lakeland District Council, but returned to the town after a public outcry and is now on permanent display at the Yorkshire Dales Information Centre in Main Street, where it is beautifully maintained in full working order. (Information supplied by Mr R.H. Thomas.)

The Sedbergh Synchronome.

# BEHIND ST MARY'S CHURCH, KIRKBY LONSDALE

## *UNUSUAL SMALL-SCALE STRUCTURES WITH A MAGNIFICENT PANORAMA*

St Mary's Church at Kirkby is set amid a spacious churchyard behind Market Street and is reached through iron gates with an arch dated '1823'. The church's exterior displays a mixture of styles and beyond its walls there are superb views of Cumbrian fells to the north and west.

An octagonal building with cement-block battlements and four arched openings has sometimes been taken to be a watch tower to keep guard against grave robbers, but this eighteenth-century retreat actually began life as a gazebo alongside the neighbouring vicarage garden wall. At a later date the garden was taken over as a burial plot and the gazebo featured in the churchyard setting.

It is claimed that W.M. Turner worked from this ornate shelter in 1822 while he was painting his 'View of the River Lune' and John Ruskin described the views across the valley of the Lune as 'One of the loveliest scenes in England.'

No doubt it was this magnificent panorama that led to construction of the garden pavilion, Church Brow Cottage, across the lane from the churchyard gazebo. In recent years it has been refurbished and operated as a holiday cottage by the Vivat Trust.

**Access**

St Mary's Church is behind Market Street at Kirkby Lonsdale which is beside the A65, between the M6 (Junction 36) and Settle.

*Above right:* Gazebo in the churchyard of St Mary's Church, Kirkby Lonsdale.

*Right:* Church Brow Cottage, Kirkby Lonsdale.

# DEVIL'S BRIDGE, KIRKBY LONSDALE

*AN IMPRESSIVE CROSSING POINT BY MEN OF GOD OR THE DEVIL HIMSELF …*

**Access**

Devil's Bridge is on the south side of Kirkby Lonsdale beside the A683 from the town to Sedbergh and Dent.

There is no exact date for construction of the fine three-arched bridge over the River Lune at Kirkby Lonsdale but it is believed to be the work of monks from St Mary's Abbey, York, who were owners of the manor at the end of the fifteenth and early sixteenth centuries.

The ribbed arches tower some 45ft above the river and triangular cut waters on the upstream pier have helped the bridge to withstand successive floods. Local stone from quarries at Hutton Roof and Newton was used in the construction of Devil's Bridge which had roadside recesses to allow horses to pass. Battlements were probably added during the seventeenth century and since 1673 an inscription has called on all who cross to 'Fear God, Honour the King.' In more recent times the volume of traffic led to the opening of the Stanley Bridge in 1932.

A number of tales surround the naming of Devil's Bridge and most feature the Crafty Crone, who is alleged to have lived beside the river. She kept her cattle on the opposite bank and reached them by wading across, but when the river level rose she could not cross. According to the legend, the Devil offered to build her a bridge overnight in return for the soul of the first creature who crossed it. After it had been constructed, the Devil waited for her to cross and forfeit her soul, but the Crafty Crone thwarted the Prince of Darkness by throwing a bun across the bridge for her dog to chase.

Supporters of the story draw attention to the Devil's neck collar, some 400yds downstream from the bridge. A large circular hole in a block of limestone is said to be the point where he flung away the collar after being fooled by the Crafty Crone.

Another version of the tale is that the Devil planned a much larger bridge, but as he was flying over Casterton Fell with a load of stones in his apron, the apron strings

Devil's Bridge, Kirkby Lonsdale.

broke and he dropped most of them on the fell side. This accounts for the narrow width of the bridge and the number of stones which lie scattered on the slopes of Casterton Fell.

# UNUSUAL ASPECTS AROUND KIRKBY LONSDALE

## *FROM AN ANCIENT MILESTONE TO STRANGE STREET NAMES*

**Access**

Kirkby Lonsdale is on the A65 between the M6 (Junction 36) and Settle.

Kirkby Lonsdale is a town of great charm with many buildings of interest. St Mary's Church, the Market Square and Devil's Bridge are the most obvious places around the township, but there are other smaller and less obvious features that add to its overall attraction. For example a stubby, rounded milestone within a simple stone shelter reads Ingleton 7 miles, Clapham 11, Settle 17 and London 250.

From the Market Square with its octagonal Tudor-style Cross (of 1905) Salt Pie Lane runs ahead to link with Market Street. This narrow roadway with distinctive frontages is said to have gained its name after a publican's wife deliberately baked salty pies in order to increase the thirst of customers.

A milestone at Kirkby Lonsdale.

A rugby ball above the doorway at the Orange Tree Inn.

Jingling Lane leads from the market square to the bridge over the River Lune and takes its name from the days when horses made their way along this route beside a narrow beck (which is now culverted below the roadway). As they moved along the lane their harnesses jingled noisily and prompted the name that is in current use.

St Mary's Church covers ground between Market Street and the River Lune and its external walls reflect a range of styles including Norman work in the lower part of the tower. At a higher level, the clock face on the tower is set at an angle (rather than flat on the wall) so that a nearby householder could have a clear view of the timepiece.

A small square on the south-east side of the church has the remaining section of the town's old market cross while on the opposite side of the churchyard, on Firbank, the colourful frontage of the Orange Tree Inn is enlivened still further by the addition of a colourful rugby ball (indicating that the landlord is a true rugby fanatic).

# CUMBRIAN CULINARY CURIOSITIES

## FORTIFYING, SUSTAINING AND ... TICKLING THE PALATE

Every region has its own distinctive, traditional food stuffs, but Cumbria, with is diversity of landscapes and long-established lifestyles, seems to have even more than most other areas.

Cumberland Sausage is sold in one long strip rather than in links and includes pork and herbs. Individual butchers jealously guard their own secret recipe and this explains the variety of tastes from one area to another. It is traditionally served with a sauce made from Bramley apples, brown sugar and a pinch of mace or with Cumberland mustard, which was originally made to meet a local demand from the Alston area.

Cumberland Ham is given its distinctive taste by desalting the hams and adding brown sugar before it is air-cured, and it is often served with Cumberland Sauce which can be served either hot or cold. The sauce is made from the juice and rind of two oranges and one lemon, which are simmered before four tablespoons of redcurrant jelly are stirred into the mixture until dissolved. Port wine or elderberry wine is often added to further enrich the taste.

Windermere Char is a little-known member of the salmon family which is found only in deep lakes like Windermere. It is traditionally eaten in a pie, potted or freshly caught and is in season from July to October.

Lake Windermere, home
of Windermere Char.

'Tattie Pots' or Tattie Pie was said to be John Peel's (*see* page 17) favourite dish and is made from potatoes, onions and Herdwick mutton.

When it comes to cakes and desserts there is an equally wide range of locally produced delicacies. These include Cumberland Currant Cake, Porter Cake and Cumberland Pudding, but perhaps the best known are Grasmere Gingerbread and Kendal Mint Cake.

Sarah Nelson is credited with making the first Grasmere Gingerbread in 1854. During that year she moved into a former schoolhouse next to St Oswald's churchyard and began to sell her confectionery – a cross between a biscuit and a cake – from a tree stump outside the front door. Sarah Nelson died in 1904 at the age of eighty-eight, but her secret recipe is still used to make and sell Grasmere Gingerbread from the old shop beside the churchyard.

Kendal Mint Cake has also been enjoyed by generations of people all over the world. With ingredients including sugar, glucose, syrup, salt and oil of peppermint it is perhaps not surprising that wrappers state it was 'carried by the successful British Everest Expedition of 1975 and by other great expeditions since the turn of the century.'

The South Lakeland valleys of Lyth and Winster are noted for their crop of damsons. Damson trees are often found around sites of Roman camps and Crusaders may have imported them from the Damascus area, but whatever their origins, damson skins were a source of dye for cloth makers in the Kendal area and they became a valuable commodity at local fairs. During spring time lanes and fields along the valleys are covered with damson blossom and a little later in the year a whole range of damson products, from wines and liqueurs to pies and cheeses, are on sale to add colour and flavour to Cumbria's culinary scene. (Details about Cumbrian foodstuffs are available from local Tourist Information Centres.)

The Gingerbread Shop, Grasmere.

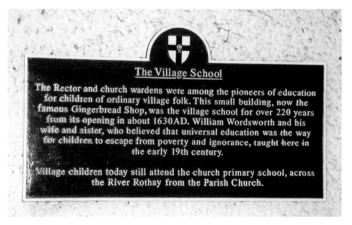

### The Village School

The Rector and church wardens were among the pioneers of education for children of ordinary village folk. This small building, now the famous Gingerbread Shop, was the village school for over 220 years from its opening in about 1630AD. William Wordsworth and his wife and sister, who believed that universal education was the way for children to escape from poverty and ignorance, taught here in the early 19th century.

Village children today still attend the church primary school, across the River Rothay from the Parish Church.

A plaque on the Gingerbread Shop at Grasmere.

*Below left:* The Kendal Mint Cake factory.

*Below right:* Damson Dene in the Lyth Valley.

# Bibliography

## BOOKS

Headly, Gwyn and Meulenkamp, Wim *Follies* (1999)
Mee, Arthur *The Lake Counties, Cumberland and Westmoreland* (1961)
Mee, Arthur *Lancashire* (1949)
Pevsner, Nikolaus *Buildings of England, Cumberland and Westmoreland* (1973)
Robinson, Cedric *Between the Tides* (2007)
'Spartina' *Looking at Northern Lakeland* (1972)
Thurston, Kat *Curiosities of Cumbria* (1994)

## LOCAL GUIDES AND MONOGRAPHS

Bradbury, Dennis *Arnside: A Guide and Community History*
Caldbeck and District Local History Society *Local Caldbeck Characters*
McAndrews, I.W. and Tedd, J.M. *St Bees' Man*
Orrell, R. *The Best Guide to Ravenglass*
Thompson, T.W. *Hawkshead Church, Chapelry and Parish*
Turner, B. *Memories of Ravenglass*
Tyson, E. *A Short History of St Mary's Church, Gosforth*

## ARTICLES

Variously published in issues of *Cumbria Magazine* (Country Publications Ltd)

## MISCELLANEOUS

Bewcastle: A Brief Historical Sketch
Church of St Paul, Irton, Cumbria
Gardens, Parks and Wildlife of Cumbria – The Lake District (Cumbria Tourist Board)
Keswick: Heart of the Lake District
Rheged the Story: 500 Million years in the making
St Mary's Church, Wreay: A Short Guide
Storrs Hall History Lake Windermere
Story of Piel Island and its Castle

# Other local titles published by The History Press

### Tees Valley Curiosities
ROBERT WOODHOUSE

This volume explores the hidden history behind a series of unusual, intriguing and extraordinary buildings, structures, incidents and people from all parts of the county. Featured in these pages are fascinating relics from the area's industrail, ecclesistical and military past including Redcar's war-time early warning system, Yarm's octagonal Methodist chapel, Thornaby's Five Lamps, Middlesbrough's Dock Tower with its three clock faces, and the intriguing primeval forests that lie off the beaches of Hartlepool and Redcar.

978 0 7509 5077 0

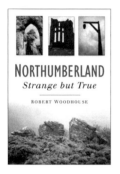

### Northumberland: Strange but True
ROBERT WOODHOUSE

*Northumberland: Strange but True* brings together a series of unusual, curious and altogether extraordinary buildings, incidents and people from all parts of the county. Using a range of illustrations, from old and recent photographs to maps, prints and engravings, Robert Woodhouse tells an entertaining story – an alternative history of Northumberland that will fascinate residents and visitors alike.

978 0 7509 4067 2

### County Durham: Strange but True
ROBERT WOODHOUSE

Robert Woodhouse sets out to discover the truth about eccentric characters, curious buildings, strange place names, weird weather, mazes, standing stones and holes in the ground. Local folklore, customs and legend are also examined to show how real events have been exaggerated and embroidered over the years. Illustrated with a range of pictures, this book is an alternative history of County Durham that will fascinate residents and visitors alike.

978 0 7509 3731 3

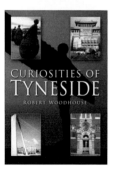

### Curiosities of Tyneside
ROBERT WOODHOUSE

Robert Woodhouse guides the reader to over 100 remarkable and curious sights to be found on Tyneside, spanning centuries of history from Roman times right up to the present day. Many of these fascinating relics of the past are overlooked by residents and visitors alike, but the inclusion in this book of location and access details, as well as numerous illustrations, means that readers can easily discover an immense variety of history, humanity and architecture for themselves.

978 0 7509 4444 1

Visit our website and discover thousands of other History Press books.www.thehistorypress.co.uk

The History Press